Behind ENEMY Lines

A Memoir of James Moffat
By Mary Thomas

Epic Press

Belleville, Ontario, Canada

BEHIND ENEMY LINES

Copyright © 2001, Mary Thomas

ISBN: 1-55306-196-9

First printing, April 2001
Second printing, July 2001

Cover photo: F/O Jim Moffat, 1943.
Halifax art by Ron Craven

**For more information or
to order additional copies, please contact:**

Behind Enemy Lines
36 Meadowvale Ave.
Belleville, ON K8N 2L4
behindenemy@hotmail.com

Printed in Canada
by
Epic Press

To
Earle Fleming

Jim Moss

ACKNOWLEDGEMENTS

WHEN I BEGAN WRITING THIS BOOK it was to be the story of a Canadian airman in World War II, James Moffat, trapped behind enemy lines in Europe. Alone. Facing danger and hardships. Running for his life, trying to get to Switzerland, and back to England. It wasn't long before I realized it was more than that. It was also the story of the people who rescued him, helped him, looked after him when he was sick. People he fought beside. These were the villagers of southern Belgium and north eastern France, trying to live under the occupation of a brutal Nazi Germany. Carrying out clandestine operations as best they could. Members of the Paul family of Belgium were the first to help James Moffat. When I first wrote to Anne Paul regarding her uncle Albert Paul, a resistance hero and martyr, I said the Moffat family owes the Pauls a debt which I hope this book will help to repay, in part, by telling of the courage of the Belgians and the Pauls. Anne Paul wrote

"...we also have a debt to pay to James. He was our Liberator." By that I understood her to be paying tribute to all the young men and women who lost all or part of their youth in World War II.

I want to thank the people who helped me to research this book. That includes my brother Jim who withstood, with good grace, my probing into his memories of nearly sixty years ago. My brother Bob Moffat for his memories of the homefront. I owe thanks especially to Anne Paul and the Paul family in the province of Luxembourg, Belgium, for providing important documents about the life and death of Albert Paul. I want to thank Jacques Sougné of the University of Liège who gave me background to *La Citadelle Sainte Walburge*. He also put me in touch with his father Gilbert Sougné of Chaudfontaine, Belgium. Gilbert Sougné, a World War II *passioné*, helped with my research into the Belgian *Resistance*, the day to day life of Belgian prisoners under the Nazi occupation particularly in *La Citadelle*, and the history of occupied Belgium. I owe thanks to Pierre Beaujean of the *Centre Liègeois d'Histoire et d'Archéologie Militaires*, Liège, Belgium. I am grateful to *Bourgmestre* Francois Rits of Halanzy, Belgium who sent me journals of the local *Resistance*. And to Anne-Marie Bradfer of the *Musée Gaumais*, Virton, Belgium, who provided a history of that museum and its founder Edmond-Pierre Fouss. I thank Robert Jones of Willenhall, West Midlands, England who recounted the history of his father, William (Bill) Jones. And a thank you to Pat for his moral support.

Mary Thomas
Belleville, ON, March, 2001

FOREWORD

FOR MANY YEARS, TO MARK THE Squadron Anniversary and to honour those who have fallen before us in the name of our country, 427 Squadron has held a "Gathering of the Lions." This gathering has also been an excellent occasion to renew our ties and friendships with present and former members of the Squadron (young and old Lions).

It was at one of these gathering in 1997 that, as the newly appointed Commanding Officer of 427 Tactical Helicopter Squadron, I first met James Moffat. Jim immediately impressed me as a fabulous storyteller and as someone who was not afraid to talk about his personal war experiences.

Jim is a member of the Royal Air Force Escaping Society, Canadian Branch. He has overcome the trauma that has affected so many veterans who have endured similar war hardships. Fortunately for us, Jim willingly expresses his own feelings and experiences as the tail gunner of a bomber crew during the war and the adventures he encountered behind enemy lines.

For military personnel, or anyone not having endured these life-or-death situations, to hear first-hand war stories by veterans is fascinating and intriguing. Therefore, one can imagine the impact Jim has had, during our annual "Gathering of the Lions," on the young members of 427 Tactical Helicopter Squadron over the years.

In the summer of 1999, British Airways organized an unveiling ceremony in the memory of a Halifax bomber crew that crashed on its land during the war. Jim accompanied me to London, England to attend this ceremony. At age 77 he appeared as fit as a 20-year-old and his memory was as sharp as ever.

His memoir is not an embellishment of his adventures, but the true story of the grim reality of war and especially the life of an escapee, hiding and fighting alongside the Belgian Resistance and the French Maquis behind enemy lines during WWII.

Daniel Guertin , CD,
Lieutenant Colonel, Commanding Officer (1997-2000)
427 Tactical Helicopter Squadron
Petawawa

CHAPTER ONE

England, March 1944

THE DREARY LATE WINTER IN YORKSHIRE, with its gray skies and constant rain, had cleared, and now the nights were bathed in moonlight. So I was surprised to hear we were going on "Ops" or operations that night. It was a full-moon period and we all assumed we wouldn't be flying.

I had just returned to Royal Air Force Station Leeming, in northern England, from a week in Edinburgh. Red Soeder and I had collected on a free holiday, thanks to Lord Nuffield. William Richard Morris was an auto manufacturer and philanthropist. He was named Viscount Nuffield in 1938. His Morris company soon became known as the "British Ford." During World War II he built aircraft. And, like many wealthy Britains during the war, he gave the soldiers a holiday away from the battle. Lord Nuffield would pay for a week in the city of your choice if you applied ahead of time, and if you were still alive to take advantage of it. Red Soeder and I had got our week in, and the very day we got back we were facing a raid.

We went through the aircraft checks and after lunch in the mess went to the briefing room with all the crews that were to fly that night. The news was even more surprising. Not only were we flying in moonlight, but the target was in Germany. Deep into Germany at Nuremburg! But it was cancelled. Next morning it was on again.

Same target. Same route. And in bright moonlight. Usually we did not go into Germany in moonlight since it was too easy for the fighters to see us. In all my other operations I had only flown into France in bright moonlight. That was to Le Mans. To Germany it would be very risky indeed. My first thought was that if there were spies about the Germans would be onto us and we would be dead ducks. At the briefing everyone was talking about this same worry. Red and I had won a lot of money at the dog races in Edinburgh. I had no chance to put my winnings, about $1500 Canadian, in the bank so I hid it in a sock, in my dresser, in the officers' quarters. I never saw it again!

Once I had checked with the gunnery section and knew that I was on "Ops" I walked across the hanger to see when the skipper was going out to the aircraft for our checkup. Our skipper, or pilot, was twenty-nine year old Squadron Leader George Laird, DFC. He already had fifteen operations under his belt. This was his sixteenth. I had lunch at the mess and headed for the transport section for the drive out to our Halifax bomber. The one sporting movie star Gary Cooper on the fuselage We all had to check out our own equipment.

I scrambled into our "kite" W-Willy through the port side, turned right where there was a small door near the tail.

I opened this, then the two small sliding doors into the turret. I had to struggle to get my feet into the tiny turret which barely had sit-down room. At six feet I was unusually tall for a tail gunner. I bent double to get my head in, then sat down behind the four guns. I checked that the ammunition feed was all right, turned on the reflector sight to see that it worked, turned the gun turret to right and left, guns up and down. I checked the oxygen, intercom and signal buttons. I reported to the skipper that all was well.

We drove back across the tarmac to the briefing room to hear the news. The plane crews usually sat together for the briefings. We all let out groans of disbelief as the target was revealed. Same target. Same route. I couldn't believe it. After the briefing I headed to my room for a rest. I had an uneasy feeling about the way this was going. And it was my thirteenth Op as well!

I lay on my bed upstairs in the officers' quarters. I had not known my grandfather. He had left his family in England at the turn of the century and gone out to South Africa. The story was that he had died while fighting in the Boer War. My father had fought in the first World War, and survived. I didn't think I would survive this one. I tried to rest. It seemed a strange way to fight a war. Eight hours of hell flying over Germany into the face of flak and fighter planes, with thousands of gallons of high octane gasoline and about five tons of bombs to drop. Then home to white sheets, regular meals, and an eight-to-five work day in the office at the gunnery section. With the pubs a fifteen minute walk away. Two different worlds.

We had supper later than the rest of the squadrons that were not operational that night. It was a special menu of poached eggs on toast. We actually got one whole egg when we were flying a raid. And I had two since George Laird was always too nervous to eat before a raid. I got his helping every time we were operational. This was about once a month. After the supper we went to the equipment section to put on heavy navy sweaters. We two gunners put on large coveralls and our electrical suits, with Mae West life jackets, plus the parachute harnesses. The rest of the crew wore the sweaters and leather fur-lined jackets. I pulled on the heavy fur-lined boots, picked up my parachute and made my way to the bus which would take us to the Halifax aircraft. Our second dickey for this operation was Staff Sergeant Art Stainton, a clean cut looking fellow on his first raid. Usually the pilots would fly three flights as second dickey with experienced pilots, before taking their own crew up.

It was about nine o'clock when we arrived at the Halifax. I peed on the tail wheel as I usually did since I would have no chance to do so again for eight or nine hours. We climbed into the "kite" on the port side. I scrambled in, turned right and headed back for the tail gunner's turret with its perspex dome. This was all done in total darkness. It was now even more difficult to get my six foot frame bent into this enclosure since I had all the extra padding on. I fastened my parachute on the wall just before entering the turret. I put my left foot in, sat on the wheel housing, got my right foot in, closed the door and plugged in the intercom and oxygen.

I gave the reflector light and turret workings another check And reported to the skipper that all was well. Then I made my way to the rest position in the middle of the plane with the rest of the crew, except the pilots and engineer of course, and waited for the order to roll. We were all a little apprehensive regarding our navigator Red Soeder because the doctor didn't want him to fly. Said he was too ill. Red had some kind of medical condition and wasn't supposed to drink. We had done a little drinking in Edinburgh, of course. But Laird said, "If I fly, my navigator flies." So Red was flying.

The pilot now had all four motors roaring and flight engineer Jock Morrison was watching the pressure and temperature gauges for any signs of trouble. The bombers all around us on the tarmac moved out of the parking area, making their way to the runways. The sound was deafening even with our helmets on since every 30 seconds or so an aircraft would take off with a roar. Finally our turn came. The brakes went on and Laird opened the throttles.

Our aircraft shuddered there for an instant, finally the brakes were released and we lumbered down the runway. The crew members sat in the pitch blackness during the takeoff. Just as you thought you might run out of runway we picked up speed and took off. This was the risky part if we crashed, and the odd one did. We had about five tons worth of bombs and about 2,000 gallons of high test octane fuel on board. I don't know what the other fellows did at take off time but I always said a little prayer.

We all returned to our positions and once back in the turret I, along with mid- upper gunner "Smitty", watched all around for our other planes that might get too close. Laird circled right over the base so that Soeder could get an exact fix on his map and start his timed run to his first navigation point, checking plane speed and true wind speed. I had to keep a sharp eye out in the darkness for planes, in case of collision. Hundreds of planes were circling from all the Royal Canadian Air Force Six Group and Royal Air Force Group airfields in our part of northern England.

Within half an hour we were flying in the dark. In the bomber stream, but seeing nothing because there were no flying lights. We normally saw two or three of our aircraft go down in flames once we'd crossed the English Channel. On this operation at one point I saw twenty in a matter of minutes. I never thought we would reach Nuremburg.

The crisis years of the war had passed. England was now packed with troops from every Allied nation and the invasion of German-occupied Europe was obviously not far away. The Allies had been bombarding German cities for quite a while now. Thousands of Halifaxes and Lancasters, led by Pathfinders, dropping heavy tonnage. Month after month Bomber Command broke its own records.

During the month of March in 1944 strategic night bombers delivered a record 20,000 tons on Germany and 8,000 tons elsewhere in the war zones. Just two weeks before this run the night force that was sent out included more than 1,000 four-engined bombers, and 3,000 tons were dropped on Stuttgart and other targets. But "area" bombing was giving way to more specific targeting and the raid on Nuremburg, deep into German territory, was the last of the "area" bombing. On this night, March 30, 779 bombers streamed across the North Sea into Germany. This attack on the city of Nuremberg, which might have been another routine raid, became a nightmare. The bombing raid did only slight damage to the city but Bomber Command had the heaviest losses of the war. At the end of the night there were 97 Lancasters and Halifaxes missing, more than 500 men killed, and more than 150 taken prisoner.

We didn't have much trouble as we headed out. As we were getting ready to cross the English Channel the pilot had to go to the bathroom. None of the other crew members went to the bathroom on an operation, but George Laird was a nervous type. He was brave but the most nervous person I've ever met. He was scared stiff all the time, which is why he couldn't eat before flight time. We had just reached the coast of England and started out over the channel. He said, "O.K. engineer, give me the bottle," and we knew what kind of bottle he meant. Then a little later I heard Pat Clapham, the wireless operator, say, "Skipper, I think we have an oil leak." I could just visualize him checking in the darkness whether or not it was oil. Then, "Oh, you bloody bastard. You pissed all over me, and you've shorted out the "G" and you've shorted out the H2S." Our navigational equipment. "And my wireless is all shorted out."

Shortly after this the navigator, Red Soeder, found that the winds were apparently fifty miles an hour faster than had been broadcast for the raid. Some aircraft, with expert navigators on board, were designated "wind finders." They had broadcast that the winds were fifty miles an hour at 15,000 to 20,000 feet. Soeder found them to be 100 miles an hour. When he reported this the "wind finders" jumped in with a compromise, "We'll broadcast them at eighty mph. One hundred mph can't be correct." As a result of this muddle, a large number of the bombers hit Schweinfurt instead of the target Nuremburg.

Most of the aircraft, at least a lot of them, were about a mile or two north of us. And they were being shot down in flames by German fighters. An easy target because of the bright moonlight. There was a high thin cloud and we were silhouetted against it. An easy target for the German fighters. The gunners usually reported each aircraft that went down, and its direction. The navigator would plot it so that the base would know where these planes had crashed. I got up to twenty-two aircraft within about twenty minutes and Laird said, "That's it. Report no more. Just keep your bloody eyes open for fighters." It was quiet in the plane from then on. I still saw a lot of planes go down. About eighty aircraft were shot down, most of them before we got to Nuremburg. The maximum we'd lost before then was maybe seventy during a whole raid. We got to the target, at least where the target should be visible and we couldn't see anything. Navigator Red Soeder said, "Well, fly another ten minutes and then you have to turn to starboard." The mid-upper gunner couldn't see anything. The bomb-aimer couldn't see anything. It was just dark out there. We turned and all of a sudden the pilot said, "I think I see it. I think I see it. I see some colour up ahead."

We approached. The target was supposed to be clear but it was nothing but cloud. We could see a glow down under the clouds. We flew over the target and there were no target markers. We decide to bomb the centre of the glow. There was only one other bomber over the target about a mile to our port. I saw a German fighter, a Messerschmidt 109 diving down at the other Halifax. Either the Halifax gunners killed him and he ran into the bomber, or the German fighter pilot miscalculated. He dove in and cut off the tail of the Halifax. The two planes crashed.

We dropped our bombs and headed home. No flak. No fighters in sight. My doomsday feeling was gone. As I looked out from my turret there was darkness all around. About an hour later the navigator broke the silence. "I'm sorry George," he said to our pilot. "I've made a mistake. I'll give you a new course in a minute. We're going to have to turn forty-five degrees to port to gain the track." We were off the course taken by all the other bombers. Soeder had re-calculated the course when he found out the wind speed was wrong on the way out to Nuremburg, but had forgotten to adjust for the home flight. Now he had to adjust to get us back into the bomber stream for the "back to England track." We would be heading into a stream of about 700 aircraft at a forty-five degree angle. I thought the pilot should let down, get down to a lower level and come in slower. But Laird wanted to stay at the same level. He told the crew, "Keep your eyes open, everybody, keep your eyes open and watch." In this darkness, and with no flying lights, we would not have much time to see another plane.

Laird was the only one who saw it. About an hour later. We were still about forty miles from the bomber stream. A lot of our planes were off track because of the high winds but apparently there were only the two of us within forty miles and we were both at the same height. Laird saw it at the last minute. He yelled, "What the hell..." and then the crash. We were both flying at 205 mph, and coming in at a forty-five degree angle. It was a heavy crash. Then quiet.

CHAPTER TWO

Canada, 1939

NORTHERN ONTARIO WAS STILL UNTAMED country in the early years of the first half of the twentieth century. Miners populated the towns which sprung up around the gold and silver mines. Homesteaders, many of them veterans of World War I, scraped a living from the bush and semi-cleared land. My father was one of those veteran homesteaders. His farming dream soon burned out by poor land, short growing seasons and the depression. I grew up in that school of hard knocks. On one of those homesteads just outside Timmins, a bustling gold mining centre. I spent only about three years in school and got the rest of my education through correspondence, and from my parents. They were both well read, and made sure their children were well read as well. From my early teens I had roughed it in the bush, working with hydro and survey crews. When war broke out in 1939 I had quit my job with the surveying company and walked all night the twenty-five miles into Timmins. I took the train to Toronto, determined to join the Navy. I had studied naval history and thought this was for me. On the train to Toronto I read in the Timmins Daily Press about a destroyer that had been sunk by the enemy. Everyone had survived except the stokers. They were down in the hold and didn't get out. When I arrived at the Navy recruiting office in Toronto I told the recruiters that I'd like to be a gunner. They said the only openings they had were for stokers. I said, "No thanks" and headed back for Timmins and a job in the mines. I simply walked into the mining employment agency in Timmins and was sent to the Naybob Mine about ten miles outside of town. I quickly signed on and was just as quickly shoveling rock down in a dark tunnel. Every night between ten o'clock and midnight the miners would blast the rock in the drifts. This would air out all night. The next day we would go in and wash down the dust, and I'd start my shoveling shift. I was alone with just my miners' hat lamp for light, and a visit from the shift boss every two hours. This wasn't my idea of a good thing. After a couple of days I noticed that the mine motorman would come along and hitch up the cars of rock that I had filled. I thought, 'that looks like a nice job.' His helper was switching to the cage the next week. I soon learned this was a hard day's work, filling the cars and shoveling the crushed rock that slid from the chute over the edge of the car, onto the tracks.

My next job opportunity came about because of a serious mine accident, when the cage tender forgot his business. He stuck his head out to see if the cage was coming down and it cut him in half. I became the new cage tender helper.

The cage was the elevator that took the miners below surface, and, of course, to the top again. The small enclosure carried life up and down in the mine. And we answered the emergency "nine bells" call. I remember taking one of the timber men up in an emergency. He was crying "my teeth, my beautiful teeth." The timber men built the wooden tunneling. He had been looking at the ceiling of a stope and a piece of rock fell, hitting him in the mouth, knocking out most of his teeth. Another day we brought out a miner who had been gassed. The other miners laid him on the floor of the cage. His face was purple and all the way to the surface I wondered, 'Will he live?' He did.

Eventually Roger Fournier became my helper. We became close friends. Roger had movie star looks. The dark hair and eyebrows and smooth good looks of a young Cary Grant. He wore turtleneck sweaters and a soft wool cap. He would pose with arms folded and ankles crossed, leaning against a wall. His perfect white teeth flashed in a Hollywood smile. We often went skiing together. Elda was his girl friend. Down in the mine we would test our strength. I would tighten my stomach muscles. Then Roger would thump me.

A few months later I had to go down into the drift, during the midnight shift. My job was to turn on the air blower to get rid of gas after the blast. This time the dynamite blast had bent the air system and I couldn't get it going. I stumbled back to the cage and yelled at Roger, "Ring nine bells and take me to the surface." Then I passed out. Roger carried me to the cage and took me up to the surface. I woke up flat on my back with the shift boss holding smelling salts under my nose. Roger Fournier had saved my life. I thought of that a couple of years later when flying over Germany.

I got used to running that cage. I hadn't been afraid even the first time I went down into the mine, but it was strange, very strange. Water dripped from the tunnel ceiling and ran down the walls. And the darkness. The only electric lights were at the stations. Otherwise we depended on the battery lamps on our helmets.

I was now working seven days a week at the mine. I worked that schedule for almost all the two years I was there. You weren't supposed to work alone but we got paid an extra dollar a day "risk money" so I was now working the cage alone. Old Ernie Horricks who worked the shift after me was a great drinker and never came in to work the day after pay day so I would work his shift as well. I would put in 16 hours underground, have five hours sleep, then go down for my regular shift again.

The war had been on for a couple of years now. Roger Fournier and I had decided to join the Air Force but I was turned down because I didn't have the high school graduation certificate. So Roger headed out west for training and I headed back down into the mine.

But six months after Roger joined up I saw in the Timmins newspaper that you could get into the Air Force if you had the "equivalent" of a high school education. My parents had always read to us and gave us what was virtually an expanded home education. Armed with this, I quit my job again and rushed to North Bay to sign up. The recruiters said, "Your education's not exactly what we want but you could be ground crew." I said, "If I wanted to be ground crew I'd have joined the Army." I never gave any serious thought to the Army. I didn't want to be mucking about in the mud. And my father's stories of a hard life in the army of the first World War turned me against it. The recruiter said, "Well you could be a gunner." I said, "That's what I want."

This was in March of 1942 and I was told to come back at the end of September. Once again in my enthusiasm to join up I was without a job. I couldn't get back my regular job on the cage at the Naybob but I was hired to work underground with an old Italian miner. I worked on the drilling machine in a stope. I had sold my winter parka to a Mr. Shrier when I'd gone to North Bay but now wanted it back. Unfortunately Mr. Shrier had fallen down a shaft and died.

CHAPTER THREE

MY INITIATION INTO LIFE in the service was a rude awakening for a naive guy from the north. The manning depot was in the old "cow palace" at the Canadian National Exhibition grounds in Toronto. I arrived at about nine o'clock at night and put down my baggage with the rest of the group. After we had eaten I went to collect my baggage, only to find that my camera had been stolen.

This was boot camp. We were herded together in the barracks which had about 500 bunk beds. I had a top bunk. Our home for a couple of months. Every morning we went for a two or three mile run. The rest of the day was spent square bashing, marching up and down and learning to obey commands. There was a fellow from Sudbury called Balls. The corporal would yell, "For God's sakes Balls, you're the only one in step." I thought I was in heaven. Life had just begun for me.

We moved on to Dunnville in southwestern Ontario on

ground duties at the Service Flying Training School. And to await our course start. Some New Zealanders were there taking navigational training on the Anson aircraft, and flying Harvards. One of the New Zealanders offered us a flight. Here I was in the Air Force and I'd never been in the air. What a chance. We flew out over Lake Erie. The pilot said, "I wonder how thick the ice is?" He lowered the wheels and we bumped several times on the ice. I was sold on flying. A few days later this same pilot tried another trick. He was going to knock over haystacks. The first haystack he tried was almost solid ice. He crashed and was killed.

It was at Dunnville that I picked up my lucky charm. It was New Year's Day and the traditional mess dinner at which the officers served the non-commissioned ranks. Someone had told me it was good luck to get the tip of an officer's tie. So at the first opportunity I clipped off the tie of the officer serving me, and tucked it into my breast pocket. I had this as a good luck charm throughout the war.

The Royal Canadian Air Force station at Trenton was our next stop. We began our training in navigation, gunnery, and wireless. I began teaching a bit. One fellow called Matthews was having a hard time learning about guns. He said, "If this was a cow, I'd understand it. But a gun I can't." So after hours I would go down to the gunnery section and teach the recoiling portions of the Browning machine gun to a number of the other airmen. The motto was "Trenton is at the centre of the Air Force" and "Co-operation made the Air Force what it is today."

By the time the leaves were on the trees that spring of 1943, about forty of us from the course were formed into a precision marching squad on campus at the University of Toronto. We did seventy-five movements, all in sequence, without a command. We would do this routine at banquets and various functions. We were the hottest thing on campus. Me, at the University of Toronto. Not bad for a miner from Timmins whose only high school education had been practicing with a Scottish pipe band in the basement of Timmins High!

We were posted to Number Three Bombing and Gunnery School, Macdonald, Manitoba. This was more like the real thing. At the aerodrome we flew out over Lake Winnipeg to practice shooting at a drone. One day I was firing away and the gun stopped. I reported the stoppage to the pilot and he said, "O. K. We'll abort," and headed back to the field. I realized then that I had allowed the shells to collect and this had stopped the gun. I thought, 'Oh, my God, I'm going to get bad marks for that. What is another number two stoppage? Ah, a broken cable.' It took me the fifteen minute flight back to the aerodrome to break the cable. The training sergeant said, "Did you find the problem?" I said, "Yeah, a broken cable." And I got full marks.

We had a turret simulator mounted inside a building which we used for night firing practice and you could watch the tracers out over the lake. One night the fellow who followed me in the turret was a guy called Neil. Neil spent most of his time gambling and was a bit careless. He let the turret come round into the building. Everyone hit the floor. The sergeant grabbed the turret and yelled like hell at Neil. Neil was one of the characters of the course. He knew that I didn't go out drinking. I was still studying hard. So he came to me and insisted I hold half his pay. " Even if I come to you at three o'clock in the morning, go down on my knees and beg, don't give me any money." Sure enough he woke me up the first night after pay day. "I'm on a roll. All

I need is ten dollars, Jim." I said, "No way." It was that way all through the course. Neil playing craps, losing money, and leaning on me for some of his cash.

The plane we flew in for air to air gunnery was a Fairey Battle, a light bomber There was just one tiny turret. The engine fumes would come up from below. One day this made me ill so I put my head close to an open spot near the gun and vomited. In seconds this ran out to the tail, came flying back and poured all over me. One day I was waiting down below as we came in for a landing. The guy up in the turret fainted and fell down on me. I thought it was the fumes again. When I scrambled up to get to the intercom the pilot yelled, "We've hit somebody." Two Australian airmen had been walking across the tarmac, carrying a box of ammunition. The propeller killed one, and cut the arm and leg off the other. The men had been wearing their flying helmets while on the tarmac, which was against regulations. They couldn't hear the aircraft approaching and paid the price of their mistake.

I graduated from Macdonald on June 25, 1943. I was second in the class of one hundred and twenty-two. We all got our sergeants' stripes. A lot of people had relatives at the graduation. I had no one.

The next day we were on the train back to Ontario, on leave before heading overseas. My mother was living in southern Ontario by then, in Northumberland county. Two days after I arrived home the telegram came, announcing that I was a commissioned officer. I borrowed a car and drove to Bowmanville, where my friend King Cole lived. King was a tall, stocky fellow. Handsome, with dark hair and clear skin. He and I had been the studious ones at Macdonald. We'd spend time talking, but passed on any of the wilder activities of the others. We headed to Toronto. Six of us got our commissions. I was now Pilot Officer Jim Moffat. We went to the manning depot in Toronto but there was no time for new uniforms. We were given white arm bands to wear as our officers' designation. We boarded a train headed for Halifax, four of us wearing the white arm bands. The other two officers were posted elsewhere, the rest were all sergeants.

Halifax was alive with service men and women all awaiting embarkation. I was excited. I went to the store for my new uniform which would be ready that afternoon. I was walking on air and not paying attention. I was half way down the corridor of the barracks before I realized there were women in underwear all around me. I had inadvertently walked into the Women's Division barracks. The rule in Nova Scotia at that time was that you could buy one 12 ounce bottle of liquor. It fit right into your pocket. Your plastic identification card would be stamped for the one bottle. I wiped off the stamp, went to the back of the line, got another for the other pocket and headed for a dance on the outer edge of the city.

Our stop in Halifax was only for two or three days. We marched down to the harbour wearing our steel helmets, carrying kit bags, with pistols at our waist, gas masks hanging 'round our necks. People crowded along the street, the kids waving. It all seemed glorious to me. We boarded the *Ile de France* for the voyage overseas. And there they were, the New Zealanders from Dunnville.

The day I was orderly officer on board the *Ile de France* convinced me that all my hard work at studying had paid off. We had been accommodated four to a cabin, with white sheets. We ate in the main dining room with tablecloth, silver, soup and fish. As orderly officer I had to inspect the lower ranks' accommodation. A sergeant, one of my classmates, came to escort me. He said, "I'll take you down, sir," which sounded quite nice to me. The "sir" I mean. Down below there was a long hall with hammocks slung over the tables. In one hand the airmen held their plates with mashed potatoes and hash beef. In the other they jammed a bun and a mug of coffee or tea. Then they moved along to sit at the picnic tables. I said, " Oh, my God, I'm in white sheets and you sleep in hammocks." The sergeant said, "Oh, you should see our bathroom." I walked to the stern of the ship. There was an open space with a board across. Little seats were cut into it. As you sat on the seat you could see the thrashing propellers about thirty feet below. The sergeant said, "In stormy weather the sea splashes right up here to wash us off."

I used to walk a couple of miles a day aboard ship. The men played craps. Of course, Neil lost all the money that I wasn't taking care of. The *Ile de France* wasn't in a convoy, just all by itself, weaving its way to Britain. We went north toward Iceland and saw no enemy ships. No enemy action at all. A B-24 Liberator of Coastal Command met us near Iceland. The plane exchanged messages with our ship by Aldis Lamp, flew around for about twenty minutes then resumed its submarine hunt. We disembarked at Greenoch, Scotland, near Glasgow, immediately boarding a train for Bournemouth in the south of England. This was something else. We bunked at the Westcliffe Hotel and ate at the Eastcliffe. We would march down the hill then across town and up a bit to the Eastcliffe. There were several spoons, forks and knives at each place on the table. I just kept my eye on everybody else and used what they used. We would then pick up a demi-tasse of coffee or tea and stroll into the garden to say, "How are you today?" to each other. It was all very British, and I loved it.

This was a holding station. Many of the airmen spent two or three months waiting for operational training or cross country escape training. I missed all that. I missed escape training! About the fourth day the call went out for volunteers to go straight to the squadron. They were looking for volunteers from the top of the class. I stepped forward. King Cole stepped forward, along with Stewart and others. I wanted to get to a squadron before the war was over. I was eager to get going.

We arrived at Topcliffe, Yorkshire, 1659 Conversion Unit in August of '43, Cole, Stewart, and I. I shared a room with Pilot Officer Jack Findlay, who was also a tail gunner. Findlay had been training on Wellingtons with a crew. He said, "I'll introduce you to our pilot and you can see if you want to join our crew." At this stage of the war you were able to sort out who you were going to fly with. It was important that you clicked since you would be spending dangerous times together, and your life depended on it. You all had to get along well. In the mess, three flight lieutenants were talking together and I thought I'd like to join Don Arnott's crew but Kenneth Cole, known to us as "King" Cole, was talking with him and had agreed to fly with his crew. He went to 405 Squadron as a gunner. George Laird was another pilot there. I said, "Fine, I'd like to join you. Where's the rest of the crew?" They weren't in the mess, because the rest of our crew were all sergeants. I would have preferred the navigator to be an officer. If he'd received top marks in training he'd likely have a commission. As it was our navigator wasn't bad. The problem was that the pilot was on his back all the time and the navigator would get flustered and come up with some disastrous results.

In this training section about half the airmen were Canadians and half British. I recognized the Yorkshire accent which was probably still slightly in my mother's speech. She was from Pontefract, Yorkshire. It was comforting. Our training began and we were doing circuits and bumps on the Halifax bomber. Squadron leader Bob Turnbull was teaching our pilot, Laird, how to fly the Halifax Mark V, so we did get some time cross country. It was an old crock of a plane that was just ending its career and dangerous to fly even doing circuits and bumps. Once as we were coming in and our skipper closed the throttles on all engines, the port outer engine kept on at full power. We left the runway and careened across the grassy ground finally coming to a stop. Laird called the tower "S-Sugar clear of runway, and how." We also practiced fighter plane evasion. The aircraft we used had an old Boulton Paul mid-upper turret. The Boulton Paul Defiant had been a fighter plane with a turret on the back. It had been far from successful and was scrapped. The turrets had then been used on some of the old Halifaxes. It had openings at the rear for bailing out. One day I forgot that we were travelling at 150 miles an hour and stuck my arms out to feel the breeze. That was a mistake as my arms were forced backwards and it felt like my back was breaking.

This was August of 1943 and the war news was bleak. We would read the Daily Mirror every day. We never missed the comic strip "Jane" with her cavorting around in underwear. But the rest of it was far from funny. In the mornings the British Broadcasting Corporation recounted the bomber raids along with the count of how many of our aircraft failed to return. We were losing in North Africa. The Russians were being slaughtered. I looked back to Macdonald, Manitoba where I had prayed that the war wouldn't end before I got over here. Maybe I'd prayed too hard.

Our pilot Laird was twenty-nine years old. He had worked for two years training other pilots at Brantford, Ontario before heading overseas. He knew everything, and how to do it, but he didn't work with his crew as closely as some sergeant pilots did. He would often be with the Wing Commander, polishing his apples. We had to wait a bit for a squadron assignment simply because he wanted to be an assistant flight commander so that he wouldn't lose his rank. Here he was, an assistant flight commander, and he hadn't made a trip yet.

Finally we were posted to the Royal Canadian Air Force Station at Leeming in Yorkshire. There were two Bomber Command groups in Yorkshire. Leeming was part of 6 Group which had six airfields in the Vale of York and one just over the county border in Durham. Its fifteen squadrons were all Canadian. Each Canadian squadron had a name in its title. Most of these were Canadian cities or our country's wild animals but 427 (Lion) Squadron, which I joined, was adopted by Metro-Goldwyn-Mayer Studios of Hollywood whose emblem was also a lion. The names of movies stars were painted on the fuselage of our planes. Members of our squadron were given special passes for free seats at any M-G-M movie.

Our crew started doing bull's eye training. About fifteen aircraft would fly at 10,000 feet which is a nice height. You can even see the cars on the roads below. We did a circuit to the north of Scotland, across to the Irish sea and down over Wales. One time the navigator asked me to come up and try shooting the stars. There was a bubble horizon sextant. I shot the stars and read off the figures to him just for fun.

My buddy Vanderkerckhove, a Halifax pilot, owned a motorcycle. "Why don't we go up to Darlington and have a few drinks," he said one night. Flying Officer George Pierre Vanderkerckhove was just twenty-one years old. He had been awarded the Distinguished Flying Cross early in August. He had already put in twenty-nine Ops, only one more to go before he ended his tour. He was confident. It was bright moonlight. He turned off the motorcycle headlights and we raced at about seventy miles an hour up the north road to Darlington. We arrived safely at the pub. Vanderkerckhove was killed in action over Leipzig on his thirtieth Op that same month, on August 31, 1943.

I was still the mid-upper gunner. Jack Findlay was the tail gunner. Flight engineer Bill Cardy joined us. Sergeant Bill Cardy had been in England a couple of years working as an aircraft mechanic before re-mustering to air crew. Our pilot, Flight Lieutenant Laird made three operational flights with experienced pilots before going out with his own crew. On September 5, 1943 we were ready and our target was Mannheim, Germany. It was just three weeks short of a year since I'd joined up in North Bay. I was thrilled to be finally heading out on a real operation.

Chapter Four

BEING AN INEXPERIENCED CREW we were in the fifth wave of bombers on the Mannheim operation. From about fifty miles away we could see the city on fire. The idea was to bomb the industrial area of the city, and we had specific factories we were to hit. About then we lost a motor. Not exactly lost it, but it jumped to 6,000 revs from 2,400. I could see the wings flapping. The whole aircraft was shaking. We started losing height because of the drag. Laird yelled, "Where is that damned flight engineer?" A calm voice came back over the intercom, "That damned flight engineer is right behind you, skipper." Cardy was a cool customer. He found that the constant sweep unit had malfunctioned. He eventually got the propeller feathered and cut the engine.

We were now on three engines with a heavy bomb load. We were losing height fast. Laird called out on the intercom, "What are we going to do fellows? Should we drop our bombs and head home, or should we try to make it to target?" It was like one voice, "We came all this way, let's go and bomb the target." We were anxious to get our first Op in. We hadn't come all this way, and risked our lives for nothing. We ran right up on the aiming point, flying at 10,000 feet instead of the assigned 21,000. Every wave of aircraft was assigned a specific height and time to bomb. We had to be careful not to bomb our own aircraft below us, and of course, to watch above so that we didn't get bombed on. We ended up in a flight of about thirty Stirling aircraft. They must have been surprised to see the lone Halifax. There was no flak at that height. All the flak was exploding at 20,000, and that's where the German fighters were. From my vantage point in the mid-upper turret I could see everything. It was bright as day. I never fired a shot. In fact I never fired my guns at the Germans on any of our operations.

On our way back from Mannheim we were flying on three engines and short of petrol. We had to make an emergency landing in the south of England because we were almost out of fuel. We landed at Boscome Down and flew back to Leeming the next day in another aircraft, "Z" Zebra, since ours was unserviceable. Bomber Command figured that if we lost no more than three percent of the aircraft every trip the supply of bombers and airmen could be met. That night we had lost six percent.

I was thrilled to have finally gone on our first bombing raid. It was clear in the letter I wrote home two days later. "Well it happened Mom at last I got what I have been waiting for. We bombed Mannheim the other night and let me tell you this, it is not like what I thought it would be, it doesn't matter how much I try to explain I couldn't give you an idea of what I saw or how it was. Lots of lads have told me what to expect but you can't picture it at all... then when you see the target there is at first a small red glow down in front and you never seem to get to it and then at about 20,000 feet you see down below a hell of a lot of fires, in fact it looks like molten metal with smoke coming from it and two or three cones of search lights about thirty lights in the area. But we had some bad luck going into the target our motor went and we lost about 4,000 feet before we could drop our bombs. I saw three fighters they didn't see us though I also saw two kites (aircraft) go down they are held in a cone of searchlights for a while and then you see tracer machine gun fire and he goes down in flames but the whole thing doesn't seem to be real just like toys.... Well Mom say hello to Charlie (Charlie Charron a World War I veteran and friend of the family) for me and tell him I am giving the Jerries hell, it is different this time, one night we are over Germany fighting and next we are dancing at some dance hall or in a nice billet or to a show or a pub. Sort of hard to get used to it. Best of luck be seeing you in a year or two. Don't worry about me I am over 21. Adios Jim."

On September 22 our operation was to Hanover. It was a piece of cake, no trouble at all for us. But not so easy for some, our losses were 3.7 percent. I was really uncomfortable in the turret that night. My battle dress was in the cleaners and I had to wear my number one blues. This meant my escape kit was in my hip pocket and I sat on it all the way.

Bill Cardy invited me to join him at a family wedding at Epsom Downs. His brother Joe was a major, a chaplain in the army, the Essex Scottish. His other two brothers were in the Lorne Scots. And he had an army brother-in-law, Captain Ken Cross. As the only airmen Cardy didn't want to face all those army types alone, most from the station at nearby Aldershot. The bride was English, from Epsom Downs. Lovely wedding in the local church and reception for about 100 guests under a gay marquee in the backyard of the bride's home. A great spread for a wartime do. About 90 percent of the males were in kilts.

When it was over a tall major in the Essex Scottish staggered to the railway station with us. We stopped at the Spread Eagle for a few more drinks. He took the last train for the Salisbury Plains but there were no more trains for us. Cardy suggested we sleep in the park. "Sergeants may sleep in the park, but officers don't," I said. "Let's go see if the police can help us." The police officers were willing to put us up in a cell but their sergeant vetoed that. Then a little bald headed officer came on shift. "No problem," he said. "My wife was killed in the blitz and my son and I live in the house. When I come off shift I'll get your breakfast." We woke up the next morning to the smell of bacon frying. I gave him all my clothing coupons.

It was on our third operation on October 3 that we ran into some real trouble. This trip was to Kassel in the Rhur Valley. Just as we got to the Dutch coast over the island of Texel we heard the Monica, our radar, going bip, bip, bip. We looked down, all darkness. We looked up, the bright moonlight. We couldn't see a thing. We did some dips and dives but couldn't see a fighter. Laird put over on one wing, then the other to let me have a look beneath. Nothing. The tail gunner didn't see a thing. We knew he was there because the Monica was bipping, but couldn't see him because it was dark and hazy.

It was a German fighter and he hit us full blast. It was like a handful of frozen peas thrown against a tin roof. But heavy peas. The fighter had come at us at a queer angle firing canon shells and armor-piercing ammunition. Our Halifax shook. Fire from the bomb bay shot about 300 feet out from underneath. I called out to the skipper. He said "Hell I can see it from up here." I could barely see for the flames and smoke, but directed the skipper as he took evasive action. I had such a feeling. I was so proud that I was able to function properly, knew what to do and could do it, alerting the pilot to the fire and giving evasive action advice. This was no small matter since the fighter was still out there. We were on fire and easy to see. And my job was to defend our plane.

Laird asked the navigator for a "reciprocal heading". That put us opposite to what we had been flying, so we could make base. Our incendiaries (bombs) caught fire. The ship was a flying bonfire. Laird put the plane in a stiff dive four or five times, putting out the blaze. We carried a number of 500 pound phosphorus bombs so this was important. We had dropped 5,000 feet and were heading for home again. Laird put the call out, "Are you O.K., are you O.K.?" His call to Jack Findlay, the tail gunner got no answer. I said, "I think maybe Jack is dead because I can see parts of the turret sticking up in the air."

Laird asked the bomb aimer to go back and check on the wireless operator, who wasn't answering, and on the tail gunner. "I'm at the wireless operator and he's dead." Then a little later, "I'm at the tail gunner and he's dead." The bomb aimer came back up and told the pilot, "Engineer Cardy is lying down on the deck. He seems badly hurt." The bomb aimer, twenty-four year old Sergeant Joe Corbally, bandaged up the engineer's arm as he lay unconscious on the deck. Corbally called, "Cardy's coming 'round. He's hurt but he seems O.K." Laird said, "Go drop our bombs." By this time we were over the English Channel. Corbally did his best to open the bomb bay doors, but they were stuck. The hydraulics were shot up. Cardy had taken shrapnel in one eye as well as one in his arm but he was alert and giving instructions. "There's an emergency lever but we'd better not use it. We'll save that lever to lower the wheels because you can use it to pump them down." Laird decided to carry on. He asked Corbally to fire the colours of the day since the wireless operator was dead and we couldn't turn on the I-F-F, the 'identification, friend or foe' system.

There was a fighter plane coming up behind us and the Monica was bipping again. We thought it was a British fighter since we were approaching the coast so Laird gave the order. It seemed easy enough to fire the Vary pistol but there was a bit of an argument about just what were the colours of the day. It was a good thing we looked it up because we had passed midnight and the colours had changed. These were inserted, then the bomb aimer couldn't get the pistol to fire! I called up, "I'm the gunner, maybe I should try it." "You're not hurt at all?" said Laird. "No, nothing near me at all." I got out of the turret. The first thing I saw was a string of holes on both sides of me where the bullets had gone through. There were nine German bullets in my ammunition cans, and one bullet went between my guns. As I reached up to the Vary pistol I could feel the safety bar was on. I pushed the bar off and fired the colours of the day to ensure our safe passage into British air space. The idea that two members of the crew were dead still seemed unreal, and of course, only Corbally had actually seen them.

Now the question was should we land at a nearby aerodrome in southern England or should we try for home base in Yorkshire. The pilot decided on the latter since the Wing Commander knew him, knew he was a good pilot and would likely be able to land without blowing up the bomb load. So we headed north for Skipton where we'd been flying from since our runways at Leeming were being resurfaced. The first thing the Wing Commander said was, "For God's sake aim the thing out to sea, put it on 'George' and bail out." Laird answered, "I can't do that because Cardy is badly wounded and I won't toss him out. If you don't find him right away he could die. We're coming in." The Wing Commander wanted half an hour to get everybody into the air raid shelters. We flew circuits by ourselves around the airport for that long half hour.

"Where are we?" said Cardy who had once again regained consciousness. We said, "We're circling the field and we can't get the wheels down. The hydraulics are shot and the lever won't work." He said, "I can cut a pipe, one of the hydraulic pipes, and the wheels will come down by themselves." He passed out again. We had no intercom so I ran forward and told the pilot, "Keep flying around. Cardy's coming to and we may get the wheels down." We dragged Cardy over to the rest position seat where there were about ten gasoline lines and a couple of hydraulic lines. We didn't want to cut the gasoline lines because we had burning phosphorus down in the bomb load. We had to be right on the first try. Every time Cardy tried to show us the right ones he would pass out. Finally he was able to point out the right ones. I picked up the axe, swung it down with a chop, and the oil flowed. The wheels came down. I could hear the pilot yelling, "The green lights are on. The wheels are locked. We're going in." We all laid down in the rest position, and Laird gave us a nice smooth landing.

Then the whole bomb load burst into flames. Flames and smoke engulfed the plane. We all quickly jumped out. The firefighters had been at the ready and doused the fire but they couldn't find the 2,000 pound bomb. They thought it might have dropped as we touched down. The fire trucks dashed down to the end of the runaway. No bomb. They checked the cable. It was cut. One cannon shell had hit the front of our Halifax, the other cut the one inch bomb cable. One twenty millimetre shell had hit the wireless operator and the other had hit the tail gunner, Flying Officer Jack Rogerson and Flying Officer Jack Findlay. As soon as I got on ground I dashed around the plane to see how Jack Findlay was. That was a mistake. I wished that I hadn't looked. Findlay was thirty-eight, my room-mate and kind of a father figure. He had taken a direct hit. They rolled the plane into a hanger, and locked it up.

Our pilot George Laird received the Distinguished Flying Cross (DFC). Twenty -three year old Sergeant Bill Cardy was awarded the Conspicuous Gallantry Medal for bringing us home that night. The CGM is awarded to a non-commissioned officer for "extreme valour in saving a life", and is topped only by the Victoria Cross. Cardy returned to Canada to recover. We were given three days survival leave. I went up to Middleton-St. George, about thirty miles north of Leeming where two of my buddies were flying. Mcgurty and Lamontaigne were both gunners from our course in Macdonald. And they were sergeants. I couldn't go to their mess so we talked on the roadway for a couple of hours, drinking coffee and shooting the breeze. Three days later I heard that they were up on an air test, the pilot spun in, and they were all killed.

CHAPTER FIVE

OUR NEXT TRIP WAS DUSSELDORF, and I was in the tail. The skipper told me right away "You're experienced now. I want you in the tail so that you can spot the trouble, and we'll get a new mid-upper." I wasn't too happy about sitting in Findlay's seat, but it was my job and I had no hold on mid-upper. The tail turret was a much tighter fit and I had to crouch, but the scare from the last operation still held, and I wore my parachute all the way there and back. It was very uncomfortable and I never did it again. Normally I just wore the harness, with the parachute nearby, since the chute was uncomfortable to wear strapped in front of you. We took along Pilot Officer Matherley, a Seminole Indian, as second pilot, or second dickey, on this run. We were coming up on Dusseldorf in the Ruhr Valley. The flak was heavy. We were watching for fighters. The German search lights were blinding. Over the intercom I heard Matherley say in his southern U.S. accent, "Ah say skipper, what are them purty lights?"

Laird said, "Jesus Christ" and we went weaving all over the sky. It had been a fighter coming at us with guns blazing but the whole scene over target was so unreal Matherley hadn't recognized it. Unless you'd seen the fighter gunfire coming at you like that before, you just didn't recognize it.

One night Rocky Durocher and I were on duty at the gunnery section, in case extra gunners were needed. I looked up and there coming up the corridor, with his flying kit and his Hollywood smile, was Roger Fournier. Just like the old days in Timmins.

"Roger, when did you arrive on Squadron?"

"This morning."

"My God, you're on Ops already tonight?"

"Yes."

"Well, I'll still be on duty at four o'clock. I'll see you then."

I didn't see Roger at four that morning. I never saw him again. His aircraft didn't return to base that night. A couple of days later I learned it had been shot down just as it crossed the French coast. It was almost a month before I got the word that there were no survivors. All his crew died in the crash. It was Roger's first operation. Although he had left Timmins to join up six months before I did, he came on Squadron after I did. After Bournemouth Roger went to a training unit before going to a squadron, whereas I had volunteered to go directly. This was his first, and last, operation.

We were carried forward by the rush of events and life seemed so ephemeral that we learned to live for the day. We became armoured against fate. I kept hold of the thought that I would survive, even in the face of harsh odds. And, of course, I didn't want my family worrying. I was devastated by the loss of so many comrades but a couple of weeks later wrote to my mother, lines that seem carefree in retrospect. "Dear Mom, Just a line to let you know how I am getting along. Health is perfect, outlook on life marvelous, now to send a little news. You might have seen my picture in the paper by now and might have wondered what the score was. Well, my skipper was awarded the D.F.C. and our flight engineer the C.G.M. for our shaky do on the Kassel raid. You see we were shot up badly and the skipper did a marvelous job of bringing the kite back. His picture was in the Toronto Star along with three other chaps along side the Halifax Bomber just cut it out and send it to me because it is a good line shoot picture... Boy Mom do you remember Roger Fournier. Well he is missing he went for a bust on his first trip over Germany. Sort of tough luck. You see Roger and I used to work together at Naybob. There is a chance he might be a prisoner of war. Well I always say those who play with guns are liable to get hurt, but I don't play... not much else to tell you except there is quite a bit of fog around at times. Do you remember Ripon, Harrogate, Darlington, Northallerton or Thirsk. Well I go to one of those towns two or three times a week. We can get good eats at Ripon and then go by bus to Harrogate to the pubs and to the dance. There is quite a dance floor there and a very nice band also some Canadian WAAFs... It sure is good to hear a Canadian girl speak for a change. Sort of makes you think you're back in Canada... Adios Jim. PS I go on leave the 6-th of November. I am going to Somerset to a Mr. James Steel (a great uncle). Hope there is a pub down there, ha ha. Night."

It was now November 22 and we were headed for Berlin. Our pilot Laird was now Squadron Leader, and the Flight Commander, which meant we only flew once or twice a month. We all knew the flight to Berlin was going to be the worst flight of all. The approach to Berlin was terrifying. German fighters were everywhere. The night fighters would follow the bomber stream, guided by radar. But by now the Germans had a new system, "wild boar" fighters. As soon as they knew the target they would bring in these day fighters, Messerschmitt 109's. The target area would be bright as day, with the search lights and the city on fire. The day fighters would hover above the bombers, then dive down on the bomber stream. We were flying south, east, then north over Berlin. It was as bright as Broadway. Usually we wouldn't see many aircraft until we got to the target. Going into Berlin we were in a stream of Halifax aircraft, just like going down Fifth avenue. German fighters were dropping "chandelier flares" by parachute for about a mile or more along both sides of the approach to Berlin. This lit up the sky so that their day fighters could attack us on the route in, and over the target.

We turned to starboard, went west for a mile, turned again, and were over the target. There was enough cloud that we couldn't see the city, just the brilliant lights under the cloud cover. And lots of flak. It ripped a hole in our plane, a piece went right through the pilot's parachute, destroying it. We called our pilot "Turkey" Laird. He'd explode when he saw other planes dropping their bombs short of the target. "The turkeys, the bloody turkeys, look at those turkeys dropping their bombs. We come all this way and they don't go in on the target." We saw no fighter action ourselves that night. Dropped our bombs and flew home. That was the start of the Battle of Berlin. For two months Bomber Command pounded Berlin, incessantly, but that was my only trip there. November 22, 1943.

Three days later we flew over Frankfurt. The forecast called for clear skies over the target but it was cloudy and we bombed by flares. Green Australian Wanganui flares were dropped by parachute. If we dropped our bomb load before the flares went through the clouds we would be near target. It was a lousy target and the fighters chased us all the way to the French coast. We were in cloud all the way but every once in a while the Monica would start pipping as a fighter got closer. The Halifax was weaving all over the sky. The bomb aimer, tucked away in his tight compartment beneath the pilot, was getting air sick. "I wish to hell he'd shoot us down and get it over with. I'm sick as a dog." We blew an engine over France and were low on fuel. We landed safely at Wing, an operational training unit in southern England.

It was mid-December and we spent some time with cross country training flights. I was busy teaching aircraft recognition and skeet shooting. I was training air gunners, giving them refresher runs, really. We would go out over the North Sea for air to sea shooting. Laird loved to sing while he was flying. His favorite was Old Black Magic. "...darling down and down I go, round and round I go, in a spin, loving the spin I'm in..." at the top of his voice over the intercom. One day coming back from a training flight Laird said to our wireless operator, "O.K Pat, you say you live on the Yorkshire moors. Give us directions and we'll buzz your house." Pat Clapham's family had been moved out onto the moors, because the Germans were bombing his hometown of Hull. So Pat told the navigator the directions, and we headed for his house. The skipper circled low over the house a number of times. We looked down and there was Pat's mother waving a tea towel over her head in greeting.

Our December 20-th trip to Frankfurt was the first we'd seen rocket guns. We didn't know what they were. We were halfway to the target when we saw this "fireworks" shooting up into the air and bursting. I had now been promoted and was Flying Officer Moffat. For the next while we stayed home and did air testing and formation flying with our Wing Commander Bob Turnbull. After we'd been shot up and two people died during our third operation, Laird had the idea that each member of his crew should be able to step into the other's job. So on one of the training runs, I flew the Halifax. I took it through slow turns. Turn the wheel, count one, two, three, four, straighten it. Then the aircraft turned. I was in heaven.

Two Canadian army officers, from bases in southern England, joined us on some of the training flights. One of them was Cardy's brother-in-law Captain Cross. The army was preparing for the invasion of Europe and wanted to become familiar with Bomber Command since it would be providing bombing support, once that invasion took place. The pubs of northern England kept us sane, let us enjoy life a little. In Harrogate there was an old theatre turned into a pub. That fall I had become known as the guy who liked to get up on stage, imitate a German submarine captain, or sing. The Sheep and Lamb had a little American bar at one end where we would start with scotch and rye, until they ran out, usually after two drinks. Then we headed into the barn-like section. There was a piano at each end. We'd stand around a piano and sing. One night I noticed two soldiers with beautiful voices singing at the far piano. They looked like twins and sang like angels. I called to them to join us. No reply. I took off my officers peaked cap and spun it across the room. The peak caught one guy just over the eye. Three seconds later I was on my back on the floor. They were at my throat. "I just wanted to buy you a drink and have you two join our group," I croaked. They were Brits and didn't take it lightly.

"Gandy" Ganderton had been squadron leader of B-flight. He was posted to 6 Group headquarters at Allerton Park and Laird was promoted to Squadron Leader. Red Soeder had been Gandy's navigator. Red was a tall, lanky fellow from Saskatoon, Saskatchewan. A head of ginger hair topped a pale thin face. A full British moustache split the face in two. Soeder drove a little Hillman. He was a bit of a gambler and would go to Pontefract, still in Yorkshire, for the horse races. One day he invited me out for dinner. He stopped at a pub in Wormald Green on the road to Harrogate. "How are my finances today?" he asked the woman behind the bar. Red had a deal with her. He would put money in a little cigar box behind the bar when he was flush, then would come scrounging when he was out of cash.

One night Red suggested we pay a visit to Headquarters at Allerton Park to see Gandy. There the squadron leader was, on his knees in the officers' mess, shooting craps with a number of others. Air Vice Marshall "Black" Mike McEwen who headed up 6 Group was looking on. The Wing Commander walked in. He said, "Boys you're not supposed to gamble in the officers' mess. Please cease and desist." And walked out. Quietly "Black" Mike spoke up, "Gentlemen I think you should pay attention to him." Red and I decided to take Gandy to Harrogate to keep him out of trouble. Gandy could barely walk. Red called up the military transport section and in an official voice said, "Squadron Leader Ganderton would like transportation to Harrogate." Ten minutes later we were at our favorite bar in Harrogate. Gandy said, "Oh where are we?" And walked up to the bar without assistance.

One day we took the Halifax on a food shopping information run. My pilot, Laird, was messing officer, responsible for the money to buy food for the officer's mess. He wanted to go to Middleton-St. George to discuss this task with a friend who was messing officer there. We loaded up the aircraft and made the twenty minute flight with Wing Commander Turnbull in the pilot's seat, and Laird as co-pilot. Turnbull was an amazing man. In one year he rose from sergeant to wing commander. Along the way he earned the Distinguished Flying Medal, the Air Force Cross and the Distinguished Flying Cross. We stayed a couple of hours for beer and lunch, and flew back.

Our next operation was to Berlin, but we never made it. We had been flying "W"-Willies, but now we were in a "V"-Victor. This was January 20, and it was our first Op in 1944. This Halifax seemed to be ill-fated. The starboard inner engine stopped, the "G" went out, and the wireless was down. We had no starboard inner, no navigation, and no radio. We dropped our bombs in the sea and headed home. I had trouble opening the rear turret to get out. I assumed the pilot had switched off the communications with the tower and I let go with a blast. It wasn't long before we heard this message. "Would the pilot of V-Victor report to the control tower at once." Laird had a strip torn off him for foul language on his aircraft. By the end of the month we were flying the Mark III Halifax. It was a beautiful plane with radial engines, great square tail, and handled much better. We were training again, this time flying circuits and bumps on three engines.

On February 19 we flew a raid to Liepzig. This was the major rail line out of Berlin. It was an important target in the Battle of Berlin. We had Flying Officer Weiker from Kitchener with us as second dickey. He was later decorated with a DFC for bravery but on this trip he scared the Hell out of us. As we neared the target Weiker started yelling, "Fire, fire, fire." The navigator hurried up with a fire extinguisher. Then he looked up and saw a fighter diving at us. He yelled and the pilot put us over on one wing. The fighter screamed down past us. Weiker had been yelling "Fighter" but his voice was so high no one recognized what he was saying. The losses on this raid were 9.5 percent for Bomber Command, but 15 percent for Halifaxes.

By the time we got to our February 25 operation to Augsberg we all knew we were losing more aircraft on these raids than Bomber Command had estimated. We never ran at the expected 3 percent loss. Over Augsberg, Germany we lost 3.6 percent of the bombers. The Americans had bombed at noon. Our bombing began at one the next morning. When we crossed the target there were no fighters in sight. No heavy flak, just light flak, the colorful tracers sweeping the sky. This didn't reach our 20,000 foot level. The eight hour operation to Augsberg was a "piece of cake" as far as we were concerned.

By this time any run to France was considered easy going. The March 7 operation to Le Mans went well. We took Group Captain Bryans, the station commander, as our second dickey. No flak. No German fighters. We bombed at 10,000 feet, hitting the rail yards. At this height there was more chance of hitting the yards and not French civilians. Thirty bombs fell outside the target area, killing thirty-one civilians and injuring another forty-five. From 20,000 feet up we'd think everything was going well. We were hitting the target. But that wasn't always the case. On one trip, I didn't go on it, but Bomber Command dropped a load on a Berlin target and came back celebrating this fantastic raid. When reconnaissance aircraft checked later they found that the bombs had all been dropped on false targets set up by the Germans, forty miles from Berlin.

On March 18 we flew to Frankfurt again. On our return we blew a cylinder, lost an engine and were low on fuel. We kept calling "Darkie" and "Mayday." Finally the flying control directed us to Bury St. Edmunds in southern England. We ran out of fuel just as we hit ground. The next day we flew on to Leeming station.

My next operation was the night of March 30-31, the raid on Nuremburg. The losses that night for Bomber Command overall were 11.9 percent, for Halifax aircraft 14 percent, and for our 427 "Lion" Squadron 25 percent. We had twelve aircraft flying and lost three. Twenty-two men killed. The planes of both Flight Commanders, and one junior crew, went down. Of those three aircraft, and the Lancaster that our plane had collided with, I was the only survivor. The only survivor from those four aircraft. I had no idea of this as I called out over the intercom to the other crew members, following the loud crash.

CHAPTER SIX

THE PADDED BACK OF THE TURRET cushioned the blow for me. My head, and my whole body, slammed into the back of the turret. Our plane had collided with one of our own Lancaster bombers. A 4 Group Lancaster from 622 Squadron. We hit at a forty-five degree angle, with a tremendous force. Then everything was quiet. I could see the Lancaster drifting out behind us. Drifting out into the darkness. I thought, 'The poor buggers. They'll bail out. They'll get out O.K.' I tried calling up on the intercom to check on our situation. Everything was dead. No answer. We had a little signal light system as well. I tried it. No answer. 'Well,' I thought, 'I'll go up front and see how it is.' I unhooked my oxygen and intercom, opened the tiny doors in the back of the turret. But I couldn't get up forward because the little door beside the tail wheel was all crumpled. I couldn't get it open. This was hopeless so I went back into the turret, sat down and plugged in again.

I tried the intercom again, calling to the pilot and other crew members. Nothing. I put on the oxygen mask and checked that the oxygen was flowing. I thought, 'We've been in some tough times before, we'll make it back. We got back before.' I sat there. The plane seemed steady enough. I looked out to the right and everything was O.K. I looked out to the left. There was no tail section! The tail piece had broken off with the collision. I thought, 'Oh my God, even if Laird's alive he's not going to be able to control the aircraft. I'm getting out.'

I didn't realize that the aircraft was already spinning down. If it had been in a nose dive I would have realized it, and probably wouldn't have been able to get out because of the position of the dive. It was in a "tail down" spin and I was on the inside of the spin. I wasn't thinking about any of this at the time. I got out of the turret again. I wasn't wearing my parachute, just the harness. I reached for the parachute which was hanging just outside the turret, but inside the aircraft. There were wires dangling all over it. The control wires had been cut and had sprung back around the chute. I pulled the wires away and took the parachute from the bungee cords. I stood up and realized that I was standing partly outside the aircraft. I was actually standing with one foot on the rim of the turret and the other on the tail wheel housing. From the waist up I was outside the aircraft since a large portion of the plane had been torn away by the collision.

Now I could see that the front of the aircraft was up and the tail end down a bit, but I still didn't realize that it was spinning like a leaf. There was no breeze or draft on me at all. I quickly fastened the first hook of the parachute onto my harness. I tried to hook the other side and it wouldn't catch. I was going down and I couldn't get the hook to catch.

I pulled off my electric gloves, and took off my other gloves. There was a big strap and hook, the hook was turned inward. I straightened it, hooked it. I quickly put my left hand over the front of the chute and pulled the rip cord with my right hand. Then I thought, 'Oh shit. I should jump first.'

This was my first jump. We had never been given parachute jump training but when we started our gunnery training at Macdonald, Manitoba we were shown how to put on the parachute and how to leave the plane. We were told to keep our left hand on the chute and grip the rip cord in our right hand and count to ten. Fortunately I was holding my left hand firmly against the pack preventing the pilot chute from springing out and pulling out the main chute. I held the pack tightly to my chest and jumped. I was still falling with the plane. My four guns were staring me in the face. I kicked a couple of times, finally hitting the guns and went spinning into the darkness. Just like "Old Black Magic" I was in a spin.

As soon as I was away from the plane I forgot about counting, removed my hand from the pack and the parachute opened with a snap. I couldn't feel the fall. It was as if I was suspended in space. All of a sudden a big hand pulled up hard on the harness, snapping it against my body and swinging the silk violently. The aircraft just sort of disappeared in the darkness. Our navigator Red Soeder had bailed out once, and he said that at night you just couldn't tell distance. So he said you should prepare to hit the ground as soon as you jump. Remembering this, I put my feet together, bent my knees, grabbed the cords and looked down. I just had time to think, 'He's full of it. I can see plain as day. There's a big forest, a clump of trees, and I'm going to drift over and land in that clearing.' Then bang, I hit the ground. I couldn't tell as I was coming down that it was a clump of bushes, not trees, and I was already there.

Lady Luck was with me! Not only because I had moved from mid-upper to the tail. The mid-upper turret was crushed in the collision. But also I had bailed out in the most unorthodox manner, at about 1,000 feet, and landed in a small open glade about 200 feet square, in a huge, dense forest. It was March and all those maple and beech trees had branches like spears aimed up at us. I learned later that Jock Morrison, the flight engineer, bailed out. He landed in a tree and was severely injured. He lived for twenty days in Arlon hospital. The Germans buried him in the cemetery at Arlon. The other members of my crew died in the crash. Four air crew got out of the Lancaster. One landed in the trees where he died, speared by the branches. Three others got out too late. They landed near the aircraft, their parachutes unopened. I never knew if they waited too long to jump, or were knocked out in the collision.

It was about three in the morning and I was so tired. I was alone. I thought, 'Everybody's probably dead.' I was just so tired. I walked into the forest, rolled up in my parachute and went to sleep. I woke up at about nine o'clock in the morning to the sound of church bells. 'There are trees all around. I must have been really drunk last night. I'm an officer, I don't get drunk and sleep in the woods.' Then I saw the blood. Blood all over me. And on my parachute. That was a low point. I was sure everybody was dead. The war was over for me. I was in Germany. I was going to be a prisoner of war. I was blood all over. And it was snowing. I checked myself, couldn't find any injury and realized my nose must have been bleeding from the jump. I wasn't injured, not even any aches or pains. Lady Luck on my side.

The first thing I had to do was to hide my parachute and my electrical suit. The big coverall had electrical heaters. I would plug my gloves into it, and that was what kept me warm in the turret. On one raid we had a new plane. The connections to my suit shorted out on the way to target. On the way back, as we let down over the North Sea, I screamed out. It was as if someone had driven spikes through the soles of my feet. My feet were frozen. I was ordered to hospital for three days. My feet and the side of my face were frozen. I carried a scar on my face for a few months. Well, this suit wouldn't help me much now, except maybe to sleep on. I stuffed the suit, along with my parachute, under a log in the forest. I had my Air Force survival kit. This small kit, about the size of a pack of cigarettes, was issued to each airman just before boarding the aircraft for each operation. The money in the kit corresponded to the particular target and the countries you were flying over. It also carried energy pills, water purification pills, a plastic tube with drawstring for water, a small hacksaw, and a tiny compass about a quarter inch across. And a silken map of Europe. The kit fit comfortably in the breast pocket of our battle dress.

I had heard the thuck, thuck of wood chopping just after I awoke and I walked toward it. There were three old gentlemen splitting firewood in the woods, and piling it. I really thought I was in France. Wishful thinking maybe. I didn't speak French but I approached and said, "*France, France? Aviateur.*" They looked at me. Then they turned their backs and resumed chopping. I thought they didn't want anything to do with me so I'd better try to find out about the church bells that I'd heard. I turned out of the woods onto a little roadway that led from the clearing. Down the hill, in the valley below, I could see a village. Just a few houses. There seemed to be no one about. I started walking down. The hills around were covered with forests, while below I could see some farms scattered about the valley. I walked about half a mile to the village. When almost there I saw a youngster, about twelve or so. He came out of a house, heading for the field to relieve himself in the great outdoors. I approached him. "*France? France?*" "*Nien, Nien,*" he answered. That was one German word I knew for sure. 'Oh, my God, I'm in Germany,' I thought. I immediately decided I'd better take off across country where I could find a spot to open up my maps. I needed to find out my exact location, to see what chance I had of making it back to England.

I could see a crossroads with a sign about a mile off in the distance. I decided to make for that. The sign said "Halanzy." I thought, 'That's not French, but it doesn't seem to be German. Where am I? I'd better not open up my map here where someone might see me. I'd better head for the forest.' Just then a fellow went by on a bicycle. 'If I start walking across the field what's he going to think? What's he going to say? I'd better walk along the road for a bit toward this Halanzy.' I could see the village up ahead. Quite a large village.

I was feeling very exposed. Me in my R.C.A.F uniform. I was wearing my battle dress, without a hat, and carrying my outer flying suit. But I thought, 'I have to brave it through.' It was snowing heavier now. Then the fellow on the bicycle pedaled by again! This time I could see that he was wearing a uniform. A blue uniform with a red stripe down the side. Riding a bike with a bag on the side. Maybe a postman. 'If he stops me I don't know what I'll do, but if he doesn't, I'll get through the village and to the woods again.' These thoughts were going through my head as I walked right through the village. I was almost out the other side when four young men in their twenties came bicycling toward me. Now all four of them stopped, blocking the road a few feet in front of me. They called to me, "*Prisonniere, prisonniere,*" and crossed their arms in front of them as though in handcuffs.

'This is it. They're going to take me prisoner and turn me over to the Germans for the reward.' We all knew that the Germans were handing out big rewards to the locals if they turned in Allied airmen shot down over the occupied countries. And if the local citizens helped the airmen, and were caught, they would be shot. There was a big incentive to turn-in airmen. Not many did.

I said, "*Aviateur, aviateur.*" I pointed to the Canada badges on the shoulders of my uniform. They kept rattling away. I couldn't understand a word. Then I saw a fellow running toward them. "I'm here from Birmingham, England," he yelled. "I'm here to get you back to England as fast as possible. The bloody *Boche* are right behind you. Jump behind the hedge and hide." Everybody disappeared. I followed suit. I jumped over the hedge that ran along that side of the road. It was a closely grown evergreen hedge only about three feet high and about five feet from the road. I lay down behind it. The Germans could easily have seen me if they had stopped to look.

The snow fell in fits and starts most of the day but never managed to make an impression on the ground. I made myself as comfortable as I could. I thought of my cosy electrical suit hidden under that log in the woods. As the day went on I thought of it more and more. I was cold, shivering. I was hungry. My throat ached with thoughts of a drink. I'd not had even a drink of water since before we left

Leeming the night before. I could hear vehicles going by, back and forth, for most of the day but dared not risk a look. The Germans would know about the two planes crashing nearby. They would be looking for airmen. I lay quiet, shivering as a fox at the hunt, but knowing there were friends nearby. That thought gave me hope, and courage.

I had no training in this sort of thing. No escape training at all. I'd skipped all that to go straight to squadron when they had asked for volunteers. Well, here I was and I intended to make the best of it. We had been told to approach the local people if we were in the country. Get to a local farmer. Try to talk to a person working by himself so that you could run away if you didn't trust him. So once again I had done something wrong. I had walked right into this village, right through it. But I really felt it was going to work out all right. If only I could get a drink of something.

It was getting dusk and the village had quieted down. It must have been about six o'clock when one of the men of the afternoon came toward me and motioned that I should follow him. He took me to the first building at this end of the village. We went into the back door, the living quarters. The front was a bakery. It also sold beer and wine. I blinked at the light and found myself in a large kitchen. There were three or four men, one whom spoke broken English. He said, "You come in here, we'll give you clothes. You take your uniform off right here, now, and we'll burn it." He asked where my parachute was. I explained about hiding it in the woods. They would go later and pick it up. The parachute silk was used to make underwear. After four long years of war materials were scarce.

He cocked his head at me, "Can you ride a bicycle?" "Yes," I said. He pointed to one of the men. "This one, he can't speak English, but he'll go with you and show you where to go and hide. We'll come for you, after it gets dark. O.K.?" I said only, "Yes." I quickly slipped out of my uniform and into the civilian clothes they handed me. When I turned around I saw the woman of the house talking on the telephone. I had a fleeting thought that she could be turning me in to the Germans, and I think it showed on my face. Scared. But nothing happened and I trusted these men. The one who could speak a little English told me I was in Belgium. I had parachuted at Batincourt and I was now in Halanzy. I hadn't thought of Belgium. In fact, France was 200 yards that way, and Luxembourg was 200 yards over there. I was right in the corner triangle of Belgium, France and Luxembourg. In the village of Halanzy.

I was feeling better by the minute. France, Belgium, Luxembourg, any of them would be fine. And it seemed that I had got all three. As long as it wasn't Germany it was all right with me. The woman had busied around the kitchen preparing some food for me while I'd been changing. There was a little girl of about six or seven years of age, with dark wavy hair, in a pinafore and old cardigan sweater. Shyly she carried an egg across the kitchen for her mother to cook. Halfway there she dropped it on the floor. I didn't get an egg that night. But they gave me a bottle of beer. I took the cap off, took a swig, and put it in the pocket of the old coveralls they'd given me. The woman handed me a bread sandwich, with just bacon grease smeared on it. I put that in my other pocket. We went outside. Someone brought round a bike for me and the two of us hopped on our bikes. Without a word the cyclist led off and I followed. After a short time he pointed to the forest of beech, oak, and maple trees so I got off the bike. As I did so I spilled the beer. I just managed to save half of it. I walked into the woods and sat behind a maple tree. There I ate the bacon grease sandwich and drank what was left of the beer. And how good it was.

I sat there quiet and contented enough, knowing someone was coming for me. But then I heard someone. I looked and saw a man walking through the forest. And he wasn't coming from the direction of the village. I just knew it wasn't "my" someone. The underbrush had all been cut out of this part of the woods. The villagers used it for firewood. This meant I could see quite a ways, even in the coming darkness. The man, I could see that it was a man, kept walking and looking back. He was about 300 feet away. He kept looking back over his shoulder. 'Oh no. I'd better not sit here,' I thought. He looked about fifty, and he could have just been a farmer going home from work. I wasn't sure if he could see me, but I decided to look around for a better place to hide. I got up and strolled down the hill toward the edge of the forest as if I too were a farmer going home. Down near the edge of the forest was a stand of young pines about ten or fifteen feet high and about fifty feet deep along the village side of the forest. Trees about the size of my legs. 'Aha, if I stand in among those trees, anyone looking would only see trees and not my legs. They'll look just like two more trees.' So I stood there, in the pines, waiting. There was now no sign of the man.

I stood there for about two hours. Waiting. Again I heard someone coming. Again it was a man. This time a man calling softly, "*Albert, Albert.*" Calling with the French accented "*Al-bare, Al-bare.*" I looked out of the pines and I saw a little man with a beret, a big, floppy French beret, hanging down one side of his head. I thought, 'They must be looking for me.' I stepped out of the woods and called softly in return,

"Canada, Canada." He ran over to me, grabbed my hand and shook it, all the while nodding and talking away, with his beret bobbing dangerously. He was a small man, about five foot five, a sharp face beneath the bobbing beret. He was dressed in black pants and an old well-worn black coat. I couldn't understand a word. Then he started calling louder "Albert" and more talking which I assumed was telling Albert that he'd found me. I saw two *gendarme* come out of the forest. That startled me a little. They were dressed in long black heavy coats with stand-up collars.

One of the *gendarmes* could speak a little English. He had been in the merchant navy for a while. He explained to me, in hesitant English, "These two are brothers. This is what we do. We walk into France. We walk into Luxembourg. And we come back into Belgium, the back way into this little village. We stay over night in the village and they'll take you somewhere else tomorrow. And you will stay in this gentleman's home tonight." He gave no names but I soon learned that the gentleman he was pointing to was Vital Paul, the little man with the beret. And his brother was Albert Paul, the other gendarme. They looked like brothers except Albert was so much taller.

The *gendarmes* led off and the other gentleman and I followed. We walked for about an hour, circling the hilly countryside, silently crossing three borders, to get to Vital Paul's back yard which was really just down the road from where I'd been hiding in the woods. The Paul's lived at the edge of Halanzy village. We got to their back yard and to their back door undetected. The two gendarmes left and I went with Vital Paul into his back door to meet his wife. She was a young, short, energetic woman, dressed in a white blouse and black skirt. Her dark hair pulled gently back from a round, friendly face. The kitchen was warm and cozy, and Marie-Claire Paul gave me a warm welcome. She also sat me at the kitchen table and gave me a little something to eat.

Vital Paul took me to a room on the second floor. It was a small village house and the room he took me to belonged to his two little children, seven year old Anne and eight year old Christian. Marie-Claire had taken the two children to another part of the house. They were not allowed to see me. I took off my outer clothes, crawled into a lovely soft bed and immediately fell asleep. The next morning Vital brought hot water and a lethal looking straight razor up to the tiny bathroom next door. I shaved off two days growth of beard. Very carefully. I was really more afraid of slitting my throat, at that moment, than I was of the Germans capturing me. I was now dressed in a dark pair of pants, white shirt and a dark vest. I transferred my escape kit and the little bit of money it contained to my pockets. The money was a few thousand Belgian and French *francs*. The only Canadian identification I had now was my Air Force dog tags, the round, loonie-size metal discs we wore round our necks, engraved with our service number. The theory was that if you were killed one was buried with you and one was sent home to your next of kin.

The Pauls lived comfortably in a narrow, two story, row house in Halanzy, nice wooden front door with a couple of windows top front and back. And they were putting that comfortable life on the line for me. I learned later that they had joined the resistance in 1941 along with Albert and his wife. Vital, a railroad accountant in his late thirties, was in close contact with the Allies. He provided London with weekly reports of train movements and their cargoes, in cooperation with a third man, an engineer from the local mine. Marie-Claire, looking young and innocent, had actually delivered dynamite for a major resistance sabotage job the previous year. The engineer had provided the dynamite to Vital. Marie-Claire thought it was too dangerous a job for him to deliver it to Albert, 40 kilometres away. The Germans were on the alert because of a dynamite sabotage by the French Maquis nearby. Good Friday was the day chosen. Marie-Claire sent Vital to church, put the dynamite in her handbag and took the train. She was never questioned. I knew nothing of this that morning. I just thought, 'If these people are willing to risk their lives to help me then I am going to do the best I can to make it pay off.'

After my breakfast, and the close shave, the two *gendarmes* showed up again, this time with a car. They were going to drive me to Albert Paul's home in Etalle, forty kilometres north. I walked out the front door, said goodbye to Marie-Claire and Vital Paul and approached the car. The gendarme who spoke English said, "You've insulted Madame Paul, the lady of the house." I said, "Why? I've said my thank you's and goodbyes." He said, "No, no. You have to go and kiss her on both cheeks." So I went back to the front door and said my goodbyes again, kissing Madame Paul on both cheeks.

It was a small, black sedan. The interpreter gendarme, I thought of him as that, got in the front beside Albert Paul who was driving. I quickly opened the back door and climbed into the back seat. There a surprise was awaiting me. Albert Paul's wife Cécile was sitting in the back, with a baby on her knee. And next to her was an airman, also wearing civilian clothes. He introduced himself as Bill Jones. Sounded like a "John Smith" alias, but he really was

Bill Jones. And was I glad to see him, someone I could talk to. Talk English to. He was a sergeant, a wireless operator in the Royal Air Force, with 158 Squadron, flying out of Lisset in Yorkshire. He'd been aboard a Halifax III, number LW634. It had been shot down over Metz, France, just south of Halanzy.

We exchanged a few words about how we'd managed to survive and stayed quiet for the rest the trip. I guess he was thinking like me, 'What happens now? Did any of my crew survive?' Jones had been brought north to Halanzy by the French and Belgian underground system. We were both going to Albert Paul's home. There we would stay for a while. Once we had been given new identification we would be put on a train for Brussels and follow instructions from there. This escape route went to Paris, south through France, across the Pyrenees mountains into Spain, and back to England. All we knew then was that there was a plan. And Bill and I were eager for it, as we rode north to Etalle. Bill had been shot down the same night that I had bailed out. His crew survived and spent the war in German prison camps.

The Albert Pauls had been holidaying with Cécile's parents at Halanzy when the aircraft had crashed at nearby Rachecourt, not far from where I had landed at Batincourt. They had actually gone to see the planes. Our Halifax had burned on the ground. The bodies of the crew members had been found there. The Germans had warned the villagers not to help any airmen who might have survived. Obviously the Pauls, and other villagers, had ignored that warning. It was also the day when the Germans were in Halanzy to remove the main bell from *Eglise Saint-Remy*. The Germans took everything they could get from the occupied countries. And they needed metals. So they took the church bells. All the villagers had gathered near the church to hear the bells ringing for the last time. Those were the church bells I had heard! The bells that had drawn me to the village, and with luck to these resistance workers, the *Maquis*.

It started snowing again as we moved north. I could see there was no snow staying on the ground. It was melting as it landed. But under the pine trees along the roadside I could see lumps of snow. It was April first. April Fool's Day. But my luck was holding, and I had a companion who could speak English. The black car pulled into the little village of Etalle. Albert Paul drove right to his house, and right into his garage which was attached to the side. We all got out and went quickly into the house. Madame Paul disappeared into the kitchen area with the baby. The two gendarmes took us straight upstairs. They showed us into a solarium. It was a fair sized room with frosted glass all around. There were some clear glass sections above, and frosted glass about five feet high on the sides. The English speaking *gendarme* laid it out for us. "You will spend your days here. You will not look outside into the yard. Don't let anyone see you."

CHAPTER SEVEN

GERMANY HAD PUSHED THROUGH THE ARDENNES in Belgium and on to the North Sea ports in the spring of 1940. A quarter million British troops and more than 100,000 French had been rescued off the coast at Dunkirk. On board one of the British warships were the last four of Belgium's government ministers. King Leopold of Belgium made his controversial surrender to the Germans just before the end of May.

But the Belgians immediately began developing a first-class resistance movement. War-time British Prime Minister Winston Churchill said, in his memoirs, that by 1942 these resistance groups were sending 80 percent of the information, received in London, about German defenses in western Europe. King Leopold's brother Charles joined the *Maquis* in the Ardennes, and lived in hiding for months. According to the German records, 8,000 acts of sabotage occurred in 1943 alone. On June 6, 1944, the BBC message, "King Solomon has put on his wooden clogs," one of many transmitted to

European resistance circuits, set off a larger-scale insurrection to coincide with the Allied invasion of the continent.

The Ardennes is high, wide country in the southern tip of Belgium, sparsely populated, and covered with forests. The farms and villages lie in the valleys. The area around Etalle and Virton is really an extension of the Ardennes, hilly and thickly wooded. It's close to the French and Luxembourg borders and some of the people who live there speak German as well as French. An ideal working area for resistance groups.

Bill Jones and I now settled in for what we thought would be a few days stay. It would take that long to get us our identification papers. So we became part of the household of Albert Paul.

Albert Paul was in the Etalle brigade of the *gendarmerie*. There were about seven or eight of them who would go out on their bikes on various routes through the villages in the countryside. They would control such things as ration coupons, and, in general, enforce the laws laid down by the occupying German army. And, of course, any Belgian laws that would be compatible with what the Germans wanted. I'd been scared when I first met the two gendarmes in the woods. I had thought they were going to take me to jail. It had surprised me that a gendarme would be involved in the resistance group. But now I realized how dedicated they were to the cause.

Albert Paul had been in the *gendarmerie* when the Germans invaded Belgium and France in 1940. Members of this kind of police-army had carried rifles in peace time. And they were still allowed to carry pistols. When war broke out they had had motorcycles, with sidecars and mounted machine guns. They fought the Germans during the invasion. Now in

1944, Albert still had a big scar from ear to chin from a bullet wound. The bullet had struck a nerve which caused him to have headaches periodically. He had spent nearly a year in hospital before returning to the brigade.

Albert was twenty-nine years old, nine years younger than his brother Vital. He was a dark, handsome man, his back as straight as a ramrod. He was tall, slim as a reed, but unbending. His face was distinguished by a prominent nose, dark eyebrows, and topped with a head of thick, black hair. The cheekbones were high, in a thin face underlined by a generous mouth. He wore a black uniform, with red stripes down his jacket and on his police cap. The red piping continued down the sides of his riding breeches. He wore knee-length leather boots and carried a P.38 automatic pistol in a holster on a black leather belt.

Albert was what you'd call a "free spirit." He went on his regulation rounds throughout the Etalle countryside during the day. But in his other life he was the head of the resistance unit in that area, which was about forty kilometres north east of Virton. He would go out two or three nights a week organizing sabotage against the Germans. He always left a pistol with Cécile at night while he was on these intrigues. There was a Sten gun at the house. Albert told us, "If two or three Germans come, shoot them and then run. If a bunch of Germans come, just run. Don't shoot. Just run." We had already made a plan for that dreaded event. Bill Jones and I had decided that we would run straight across the field behind the house. There were no fences and it was about 500 feet to the forest. If you went down along the hedge there were little garden plots surrounded by barbed wire from the first World War. We thought this would slow us down too much.

Some evenings Albert would tell us a bit about the underground work he was doing. One time he heard about a collaborator in the village of Etalle. A Belgian working with the Germans. Albert wrote out a message, "If you don't stop collaborating with the Germans, we'll blow your house up." He wrapped it around a stone and tossed it through the man's window. I assume it worked. He would type these messages on the typewriter at his *gendarmerie* office. I'd read enough detective novels to think the Germans might be able to trace this.

The solarium was comfortable enough and we had the run of the house. The Pauls lived in a row house, stucco over brick. The only way to the back yard was through the front door, through the house and out the back door. I never, ever saw the front of the house from the outside, of course. We weren't allowed out. The downstairs was a large kitchen and living room all in one, with a "toilette" near the kitchen. Upstairs there was a long bedroom, stretching from front to back. It was communal, for all of us. Three cots side by side in a row, in the open space. That was where we slept. Just a divider separated us from Albert, Cécile and the baby.

We weren't allowed outside. The one or two days soon stretched into more. And more. Our first job, of course, was to learn to communicate with the Pauls. They didn't speak any English at all. Bill Jones and I didn't speak French. We understood just a very little. I could count to ten and swear a little. Jones had taken French in high school but he had forgotten most of it.

We soon came up with a scheme for learning French. The Pauls had no dictionary, no dictionary at all. A dictionary seemed so fundamental to a household, but they didn't have one. So we worked it this way. Cécile and Albert, would write out words for us such as "chair" and "table." They'd write out 10 words. As we learned each word, really learned it, I would cross it off the list. When I'd crossed off five words we'd add five more. So each morning after breakfast we would go up to the solarium and practice our French. The solarium was at the end of this long bedroom and extended out to the back of the house. It was actually a large bathroom. The tub and toilet took up quite a bit of the space, but there was a table and two chairs for us to use. We would study for hours, the quiet broken only by the American Air Force bombers on daylight bombing raids. We could see them from our glassed enclosure, flying over in perfect formation. Hours later they'd straggle back at the end of the raid, having been shot up by the Germans. Sometimes the odd British Spitfire fighter would go screaming overhead at treetop level.

As our French improved the Pauls would tell us the local news. We reached a point in our self-styled education where we could read bits of the newspapers. These were all under German control, so we'd get a German view of how things were going. For instance, we read that they were still holding back the Russians. This in the spring of 1944.

Now and then we would move next door to stay with the Messiens. They shared the duty of hiding us. Out the back door into their back door under cover of darkness. I shall never forget that first time. Cécile wanted to go down to Halanzy to visit her mother and there would be nobody home during the day. Albert thought we'd be safer next door. Marcel Messien was the town notary. He and his wife Rose couldn't speak a word of English. But our French was coming along. He said that he and Rose had a real treat for us. He held up two pieces of meat. I thought, 'Oh, great, we've been living on bacon, one strip, potatoes, with bacon grease poured over.'

In the morning Cécile would give us a bowl of coffee, and a sort of coffee cake. The coffee was made of roasted grain, or something, ground up. I'd hold this coffee in the bowl and think of my mother drinking her tea from a small pudding bowl, decorated with large purple plums, that she used to use. It sort of made me feel at home. But now a treat. A real treat. Real meat. Messien said proudly, "We're going to cook this meat for you." He put a frying pan on the stove, popped the meat in. I heard it sizzle. He flipped it over. I heard it sizzle again. He flipped it out on the plate. It was barely singed on both sides. We were going to eat raw meat. It was kind of blue. Bill and I and the Messiens started to cut our meat. I said, gently, "We'd like it cooked a little more." Messien couldn't understand why we would want this. So Bill and I struggled on eating down the meat and potatoes. Chewing hard on almost raw meat. The Messiens were eating and smiling at us. Then he said, "Tell me what kind of meat it is." I thought, 'What kind of meat is it? What could they possibly get that the Pauls didn't have?' We couldn't guess. He smiled. "Horse meat."

Etalle was a small village stretching along a main street, the Rue de Virton. It was not far from Arlon, the German headquarters for the region. The Germans raided the village three times while we were there. It happened one of the nights we were getting ready to go to bed at the Messiens, while Cécile was away. Rose Messien had gone to visit a neighbor and she came running back into the house screaming, "*Les Boches, Les Boches.*" Both the Messiens turned pale. We all new the danger. Especially for them. We would be taken prisoners of war, but they would likely be tortured, even shot for harboring the enemy. They ran next door to Albert Paul's. Albert came in. The three of them were rattling away in French and we couldn't catch much of it except, "*Les Boches, Les Boches.*" I knew the Messiens were scared stiff.

Albert said, "Come with me." We went back to his house and Albert led us upstairs. He took us to the crawl space over the garage that we could enter from our bedroom area. Bill and I crawled in there. It was cramped and smelly. Anytime there was a visitor to the house or a Gestapo scare we would hide in it. This time the Germans stayed in the village that night and all the next day. We stayed huddled over the garage. No one seemed to know exactly what the Germans were looking for this time, but they were always trying to find out who was running the resistance units in the villages. They would raid various houses. They raided one just down the way from the Pauls. When Cécile came back to the village the next day, from visiting her mother, she found out that one of her best friends had been taken away. Her friends were taken away and never returned. Usually any of the locals who were taken would be questioned heavily, and then sent to concentration camps or to labor camps in Germany. The Pauls' friends didn't come back and Cécile cried for the next two or three days. We stayed in our crawl space, coming out only for meals a couple of times a day.

But then the scare passed and life carried on. Albert would go to work, Bill and I would study our French, and Cécile would look after baby Monique, and cook for us. Cécile was a lively, young woman with round, cheery cheeks. She combed the waves of her black hair back from her face.

I loved to hold Monique. I would sit in a rocking chair in the kitchen, warm from Cécile's baking. I rocked the baby and sang to her. I spoiled her, I guess, because when we first came there Monique was quite content in her crib. Cécile would put her down and off she'd go to sleep. But now she wanted to be rocked. She'd cry and I'd rock her.

Cécile would tease us. Bill Jones was a slim, dark haired, quiet guy. Neat, with conventional nice looks. Twenty-three years old. He spent a lot of time reading by himself. He had a girl friend and I didn't. Cécile would say, "How come you are an officer in the Air Force and this sergeant has lots of dates and a girl friend, and you have nothing?" I would just smile and shrug. Albert was always full of life. He was the knight in shining armour, charging the enemy with his lance. He wasn't a braggart, but he loved to tell us what he did. He told us about his unit putting explosives on power lines to blow them down. And he was the fun guy. One evening when they were teasing me again about having no girl friend he grabbed Cécile, plopped her on my knee and said, "Here's a girl friend." He used to kid me all the time.

While the Pauls were continuing to hide us, and worry about their own welfare, another burden was added. Cécile's brother, René Ravet, arrived. We had been in the house a week or so when René arrived. He was twenty-four years old. René had escaped from a forced labor camp in Germany. He had made his way back to Belgium but couldn't live at home so was on the run, using various aliases and staying at various safe houses. Then he came to Cécile. René would often run messages for Albert and the *Maquis*. And it was René who had brought us the Sten gun.

Time was going by and the two or three days were

stretching into two or three weeks. With the German raids on the village I was getting more and more worried. I had a sense of urgency. I wondered if we were being stupid to stay and maybe we should try to make it on our own. Bill Jones thought I was being a fusspot. We had our false papers now and I thought we should get out. Get going. I was Charles Lebrun, a Belgian laborer. Bill was Jacques Lenoir. I had the idea that we should walk toward Switzerland or Spain. But Albert was against Switzerland. "No, no," he said. "Switzerland you can't get in. There's no hope. Spain you might have a chance. We are making arrangements. A farm lady is going to take you to Brussels. She will sit in the same car on the train." The Pauls had hidden an airman, a squadron leader, just the month before and had passed him along the line back to England. So I was satisfied. They were the experts. They had been coached by the Allies on how to handle it.

There had been two major escape lines operating in enemy territory since early in the war, south through France and out through Spain. The Pat O'Leary line and the Comet line. They were both run by Belgians. The O'Leary line had a base at Marseilles and about 250 helpers throughout France, civilians who risked their lives to move the airmen and others down the line from safe house to safe house. Pat O'Leary was really Albert-Marie Guerisse, a former medical officer in the Belgian cavalry who had escaped to England in 1940 then volunteered to work for the secret service. He organized the escape of hundreds of people. In 1943 the O'Leary line was infiltrated by a German agent and O'Leary himself was captured. He spent the rest of the war in the Dachau concentration camp.

The largest and most successful escape line transported about 1,000 downed airmen, escaped prisoners of war and resistance workers in three years of operations. The Comet Line. It was run by a tiny Belgian nurse's aide named Andrée de Jongh, or Deedee as she was known. The people were passed, by train, from safe house to safe house, Brussels to Paris and south to Perpignon. They went over the Pyrenese mountains to Madrid, out to Gibralter, then back to England by plane or boat. Dedee made many of the trips herself leading her "packages" as she called them, across the border into Spain. She was caught in a raid on a farm house near the Spanish border. Although she admitted being the leader of the Comet line, the Gestapo never believed her. Dedee spent the rest of the war in the Ravensbruck concentration camp. By the end of 1943 there were nine escape lines sending an average of three airmen a day over the border into Spain. But the overland route was becoming more and more difficult as sabotage teams and Allied bombing spread along the French railroad system in preparation for the D-Day invasion. By early 1944 large numbers of airmen were holed up in chateaux and on farms along France's northwestern coast, unable to make their way south to Spain.

We now pinned our hopes on the promised lady but for some reason there were delays. She never showed up. Bill and I never knew the reason for this. There was another raid by the Germans and we were back under the garage roof again. Albert said the Nazis were looking for a Jewish girl. We knew that an eight year old Jewish child did live in Etalle. In fact, she lived three houses down from us. She was hidden within the family, posing as part of the Christian household. As far as I know she was never found out. Innocent as we were at the time, Bill and I didn't think the

Gestapo would spend time hunting a Jewish child.

April had passed into May. It was just before mid-month. We had been in Etalle nearly six weeks. Albert came in that night. He said, "Tonight I have something special for you. A surprise. I'm taking you out of the village. Late tonight. I'll show you something." We said, "O.K." Bill and I had never been out of the house, never anywhere since we'd come to Etalle. Except of course to go in hiding at the Messiens next door.

It was about midnight when we sneaked out the back door, through the gardens and out of the village. We crossed a field and walked about a kilometre or so to a farm. Right in the middle of a field there was a shed. Albert took us in. He flashed his light around. Twenty containers, new, round tin barrels, stood before us. They were about three feet high and maybe two feet around. Albert took the lid off one. There were chocolate bars and cigarettes nestled side by side with explosives. And what he really wanted to show us, a bunch of .38 revolvers made in Montreal, Canada. We were surprised all right. Albert was excited, "From Canada, Canada." He spread his arms around. Encompassing the whole store house. "They're all full of guns and explosives for my unit." We didn't touch any of it because he didn't want any of it in the house. He put the top back on the barrel, shut up the shed and we head back to Etalle.

This had been an exciting night out for us and certainly Albert was proud to be able to show us that help was coming to his group from as far away as Canada, but it just may have been a fateful step. We never knew if this was what brought the Germans to our door. Did the Germans accidentally run across the shed and its treasure during a regular patrol? Did someone, a collaborator, watch us go out that night? Did the Germans or a collaborator see the plane drop the stuff and the Belgian resistance workers carry it to the shed? It seemed to me as if that night's trip had a connection to the events of a few days later.

CHAPTER EIGHT

IT HAPPENED JUST AT DAYBREAK. Expected but unexpected. Terrifying. I was sleeping. The first I heard was a pounding, banging on the door. Cecile was running up the stairs with the baby hanging in her arms yelling, "*Les Boches. Les Boches.*" I woke up to see my comrades already on the run without me. Cecile's brother was already out the window and Bill Jones was running toward it. They hadn't stopped to shake me, or give me warning. We slept in our shirt and waistcoat. I pulled on my pants. I had done away with my braces. I'd made a belt out of them. Those big, blue Air Force braces would be a dead giveaway. I didn't stop for my boots but ran to the window and jumped out. It was only about an eight foot drop to the garden, right into nice, soft soil. We ran to the bottom of the garden where we were faced with an eight foot wire fence, a chicken wire fence. It's thin little squares were kind of tricky to get our fingers and toes into. Jones was a short guy. He was having trouble getting over. I gave him a push and he flopped over onto the other side and started running. I climbed over. I could see Cecile's brother about 200 feet ahead of me. Jones about 100 feet ahead. We were running for our lives. The Germans had made it to the bedroom. Two of them were at the window, one with a rifle and one with a machine pistol. I heard a "wroing" go buzzing by my ear. "Thuck, thuck,thuck" all across the field. I thought, 'How did he miss my legs?' I yelled at Jones, "Let's take the hedge. We're out in the wide open." I ducked toward the hedge.

I was immediately hidden from the Germans perched in the window. The bullets were still popping across the field. I lost track of the Belgian and Bill Jones. René Ravét was long gone. He'd got the jump on all of us and got clear away. By this time one of the soldiers was running behind me. I ran along the hedge and dove under the first fence. I ran across another little garden plot, dove under the barbed wire again. My pants caught on the barbs. I was stuck. 'Oh shit. To hell with the pants.' I slid right out of them, dove under a couple more fences, and ran into the bush. And again all the undergrowth had been cut. You could see 300 feet any way you looked. My breath was running short. We'd been shut up in the house and hadn't been exercising. My lungs were frantic and telling me so. I was gasping for air and the harsh grating sound reverberated in my ears. 'Where could I run? Which way?' I looked back. He was still hot on my tail. He was carrying the machine pistol. A couple of other guys were behind him. I was out of range and, just as I turned direction slightly, two or three clumps of bushes hid me from view. I ran past the first two. An extra large one, about 10 feet high and 20 feet around, was just before me. I dove into it. I quickly crawled into the centre.

I was puffing, and loud. I could hear him coming. I tried to stop the harsh sounds coming from my chest. I tried to stop breathing altogether so he wouldn't hear me. I watched him come. I watched his feet run right by. I thought, 'Why can't he hear me? He must be puffing as hard as I am.' He ran right by and nobody else followed. I was sure the others were looking for me so I stayed right where I was. About an hour later I heard them coming. I couldn't see straight out of the bush, but I could look down and out. What I saw were German boots going by. And dog's feet. A German shepherd dog. 'Oh, my God, they're going to get me this time.' But the dog led them along. Four more boots went by. 'The dog must be following the earlier soldier's tracks. He's not following mine.'

This was about five or six o'clock in the morning, daybreak. I hadn't realized it was a "thorn bush" that I'd crawled into until the chase had cooled down. I was naked as a jay bird from the waist down. Ouch. But the fear and the pumping adrenaline had made me impervious to pain. I'd been running over the small undergrowth that had been chopped down. My feet were cut and scratched. I hadn't noticed at first but now I did. I stayed right where I was for the remainder of the day. I was scared. I was alone again and not even sure in what direction I'd been running. And I had no clothes. I had to wait out the day so I tried to rest. When it started to get dark I decided to take a look around.

I had to crawl through about five feet of those branches to get out. The thorns were about two inches long, and strong. They ripped at my skin. It had been much easier running into the bush then carefully trying to wiggle out. 'Now what am I going to do?' I realized that the roadway wasn't far and I went to the edge. Nothing. No sign of anyone. I went back to the woods and decided to stay till morning. But not in the thorn bush! It was mid-May and still very cold at night. About six inches of leaves from last fall covered the ground. I made myself a bed. I put my back against a large maple tree and covered my legs and body with the leaves. It was a cold spring night and my naked skin shivered under the damp chill.

I was fretting about what I should do next but pushing that aside was the worry that I didn't even have my dog tags. They had been hidden in my boots which I had left back in the bedroom at the Pauls when I jumped out the window. This preyed on my mind. 'My mother doesn't know what's happening to me. If I'm shot and killed nobody will even know who I really am. I am Charles Lebrun. My false papers say I'm Charles Lebrun. James Moffat has disappeared. No one would ever find out what happened to me.'

'And Cécile. Where is she now? Is she safe? What a brave young woman! When the Gestapo pounded on the door at first light she knew what that meant. She knew they either had Albert or were looking for him. She knew they would take her as well for her part in hiding us. Bill Jones, her brother and me. The Gestapo had already taken away her friends in the night. They were never seen again. And there was little Monique, that baby I had held and rocked. Yet Cécile had taken the time to run up the stairs and warn us. She could have escaped immediately out the back door. But she saved us. Where is she now? Did she get out, escape? Is she safe?'

'It had seemed as if René Ravet would get away, but what about Bill? *What about Albert? Did they capture him?* And here I am alone again.' These thoughts ran through my mind, crowding out my physical discomfort.

I finally fell asleep, waking just as dawn was breaking. A faint grayness crept over the forest and penetrated the trees overhead. That's when I heard it. "You hoo. You hoo" It came from over there to my right. Then on my left. "You hoo. You hoo." I thought, 'Thank God. Someone's looking for me.' Then I heard it right above me "Cuckoo. Cuckoo." Birds! That was a blow. At that moment I was near to losing hope. 'I can't even head across country until I get a pair of pants and boots. I'll go to the edge of the road to see if I can get help.' There were two or three gendarmes riding by on bicycles. I yelled, "*Canadien. Canadien. Aviateur.*" My French had improved and I had no trouble understanding them as they said, "Tonight. Later tonight."

I waited with anticipation. With hope. But no sign of anyone. I spent another cold night with damp leaves for a blanket. The next day and still no sign of the gendarmes. I was sure the Germans were still around and the gendarmes couldn't take a chance. 'They won't be back I'd better get away.' I'd always been a self-starter. And of course I grew up in the bush land of northern Ontario. I had worked in the bush. I was no stranger to the forest. It was late afternoon and once again I heard chopping in the woods and I followed the sound. There was a fellow near the edge of a glade, chopping down a tree. I stopped within about twenty-five feet of him. I didn't want to get too close in case I had to run. I said, *"Bonjour."* He turned around. His face reflected his shock. A stranger in a white shirt and vest, but naked from the waist down. No underwear, no pants, no socks or shoes. And my scruffy hair standing on end. My face covered with two days growth of beard. He came to me right way. He knew. *"Oh! les sales Boches.* The dirty Germans. You wait here I'll go and get you some pants and some food."

He ran out of the little glade, across the highway to his home. I thought, 'Well if he's going to turn me in I'd better make some distance so I went off into the woods. I found a place I could watch for him to come back. He came back carrying an oat bag, a burlap bag. I joined him and he pulled out a pair of slippers, *pantouffe*, a dirty, old pair of pants, and most important of all black bread smeared with bacon grease. I ate that first. I hadn't eaten in three days. Then I put on the clothes. "Come with me," he said. "I'll check the highway. If there's nobody we'll go across. I live with my mother across the road." He was a fairly young man, about thirty, so I guessed that he was hiding from the Germans too.

The little farmstead had seen better days. Or maybe it had never seen anything better. There was a tiny house on about an acre of cleared land. The bush hovered close to the edge as if waiting its chance to reclaim that land. I assumed it was about two or three miles from Etalle but I really had no idea where I was. There were no village sounds. We stepped inside the house, directly into a tiny kitchen. The mother was expecting me. She had a big pot of cabbage soup on the stove. She dipped out a bowl and handed it to me. They watched as I ate. Then the mother began digging out some money. I said, "No, no. No money. I have money." "What will you do," she said. "I'm just going out to make sport for the Germans." She immediately burst out crying and I was sorry for my little joke. These people knew just what to expect from the Germans. "No, no. I'm going to try to make my way south, see if I can get into Switzerland or something like that." She was satisfied with that and gave me another bacon grease sandwich. I put that in my pocket and left. They were good people and willing to help but they had no resources to go any further than they had. They had no connections that would move me along. And it was obvious that they didn't want me to stay.

It was dark now as I made my way to the highway. I thought that my best bet would be to head south to Virton. I felt better now that I had made up my mind about what I would do. And I was doing it. I walked all night right along the highway, heading south on La Rue du Virton. There was no traffic. It was quiet. The few night noises were soothing. It raised memories of Timmins, especially those nights so long ago when I walked home from bagpipe lessons. I was ready to jump into the ditch if I had to. But I didn't have to.

The sky was beginning to drain its darkness but the woods were still black and I couldn't see very far. I could hear some sounds and see the outlines of some buildings ahead, maybe a church. The highway dipped down into the village here and I could see ahead quite a ways. I thought it was time to get into the fields and head down that way. I climbed the roadside fence and found myself at the top of a terraced hillside. I made my way down to the first ditch. Barbed wire guarded both sides. It was still dark enough that I had to feel my way. I held the wire down as much as possible, stretched my leg over the wire and ditch, and kind of jumped the rest of the way. I continued this maneuver as I headed down the hill. More than half way down I came to one terrace barrier that wasn't so easy. My foot didn't seem to touch the other side of the ditch. I just thought it was a little extra wide so I jumped. It was a fifteen foot drop. When I sat up I realized I'd sprained my ankle and I would have to crawl.

As dawn broke, I crawled under the last three barbed wire fences and across the ditches. I could see the village plainly now. 'This must be Virton.' Just below me there was a river with a hill on the other side. I made my way to the river, crawled along a pathway for quite a few yards and found a log being used as a bridge. I crawled across this log and up the path into the forest. My only thought was to get into the woods and sleep. Which I did.

I awoke to the sound of talking. I carefully lifted my head. There were a couple of men sitting about fifty feet from me. Talking. I ducked down again and kept quiet. They finally left and my only thought was, 'My God. I'm so dry. And so hungry. I have to find something.' I started for the sounds of the village. I headed down a sandy road and came to a little house all by itself on the near edge of the village. A short bald-headed guy was working in his garden. "*Bonjour.* I'm heading for Switzerland. Which route do I take?" He was surprised but very understanding. "I was in the first World War I know how it can be. I can help you. Take this road and keep going and you will get where you want to go." This was really kind of stupid because it was just a little road into the forest. It wasn't any kind of a main highway but I headed out on it.

Somewhere along the way I made a wrong turn and ended up in a smaller roadway that went into a field. Out in the middle of the field was a dugout, a house dug into the side of the hill. A big haystack dominated the view and sheep dotted the field. I thought this was my best chance for food and water. I approached the young shepherd and his wife. "'I'm hungry and thirsty, can I have some water? I'm really dry." The shepherd gave me a cup of water. No food. "Is there anywhere I can spend the night?" I could see that he was scared. "You can sleep in the haystack if you want to," he said. "Don't come near here." He pointed to his hillside house. That satisfied me. I'd walked all day. My ankle was still hurting. So I went out to the haystack and burrowed into the hay as far as I could. I fell asleep.

I awoke in bright morning sunlight to shouts from the shepherd. "You've got a friend, you've got a friend. A compatriot." I thought, 'Oh thank God. Another airman.' I struggled out of the haystack and looked. What I saw was a little man shuffling along through the field toward me. He called out, "I am Desiré Paul. I'm Albert Paul's cousin. I've come to take you back into Belgium."

Jim Moffat, cage tender at Naybob Mine, Timmins, Ontario, 1941

Roger Fournier with Elda and Georgette, Timmins, Ontario, 1941

Roger Fournier at Mattagimi River bridge, Timmins, Ontario, 1941

Jim Moffat at railway station, Timmins, Ontario, 1941

Some of the crew after the third operation shoot up. Left to right: Sgt Joe Corbally b/a, F/L George Laird DFC pilot, P/O Jim Moffat r/ag, Sgt George Lorimer nav. At RCAF Station Leeming, England. RCAF photo.

Sgt Bill Cardy f/e was awarded the Conspicuous Gallantry Medal for his part in bringing home the Halifax after it was shot up returning from third operation. RCAF photo.

F/O Jock Morrison DFC fle at RAF Station, Leeming, England, 1944.

Part of the class, University of Toronto RCAF refresher course, spring of 1943. Left to right: back row Airmen Bogey Fallon, Jim Moffat, and McGurty; front row Opolsky, Mulligan and Dave Turbit.

1988 reunion at Etalle, Belgium. Left to right: Marcel and Rose Messien, and Jim Moffat.

1988 reunion at Baalon, France. Left to right: Jim Moffat, Jeanne Paul, Anne Moffat, and Anne Paul. Sitting in front, Louis Paul.

Crew at RCAF Station Leeming, England, 1943. Left to right, back row: Sgt Pat Clapham wag RAF, Sq/Ldr George Laird DFC pilot, WO1 Joe Corbally b/a, F/O Jim Moffat r/ag, F/O Paddy McClune fle RAF. Seated front: Sgt Lloyd Smith mu/ag, Sgt George Lorimer nav.

At RCAF Station Leeming, Yorkshire, England, 1943. The new crew. Left to right: Sq/Ldr George Laird DFC pilot, F/O Red Soeder nav, P/O Joe Corbally b/a, Sgt Pat Clapham wag RAF, F/Lt Paddy McClune DFC fle RAF, P/O Lloyd Smith mu/ag, F/O Jim Moffat r/ag. RCAF photo.

The Halifax bomber was flown out of the RCAF Station Leeming, part of Six Group, the Canadian Group in northern England during WWII. Photo credit: artist Ron Craven, courtesy RCAF Museum.

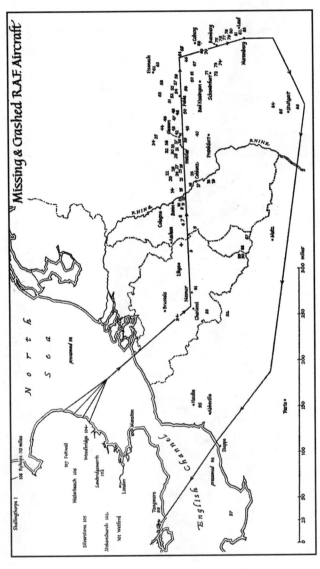

Map of Belgium—France area. Missing and crashed allied aircraft during the Nuremburg raid the night of March 30-31, 1944. Numbers 89–90 represent the mid-air crash of the two allied aircraft that Jim Moffat survived. Number 87 or 88 is believed to be the aircraft shot down that Bill Jones and his crew survived.

Cécile Paul, baby Monique, and RAF Sgt Bill Jones alias Jacques Lenoir. Paul family photo.

Albert Paul in the uniform of the Belgian gendarmerie, with Cécile about 1943.

Left to right: Vital and Marie Claire Paul, Cécile and Albert Paul.
Rear: Gilbert Paul holding Anne Paul. Paul family photo.

RAF Sgt Bill Jones and RCAF F/O Jim Moffat, alias Jacques Lenoir and Charles Lebrun. Hiding out with Albert and Cécile Paul in Etalle Belgium, May 1944. Paul family photo.

The home of Albert and Cécile Paul where RCAF F/O Jim Moffat and RAF Sgt Bill Jones hid in the spring of 1944. At left garage where they hid over-top. At right the home of Marcel and Rose Messiens who also hid the airmen.

Funeral procession for Albert Paul's reburial at Halanzy, October, 1944, after his body was brought home from La Citadelle in Liège.

L'Hermitage, Torgny Belgium. Jim Moffat hid in the belfry from about May 17 to June 1944.

Inside the belfry of l'Hermitage, Torgny Belgium where F/O Jim Moffat hid out for about a month.

Henriette and Désire Paul with daughter in Torgny after the war.

Jim Moffat spent a couple of weeks recovering at the home of resistance worker Madame Germaine Autphene, Couvreux Belgium in July of 1944. Left to right: Germaine Autphene, Jim Moffat (Charles Lebrun), Guy Giot (Emile), and friends. Autphene family photo.

The reunion. Left to right: Germaine Autphene, Jim and Anne Moffat outside Madame Autphene's home and school at Couvreux Belgium 1988.

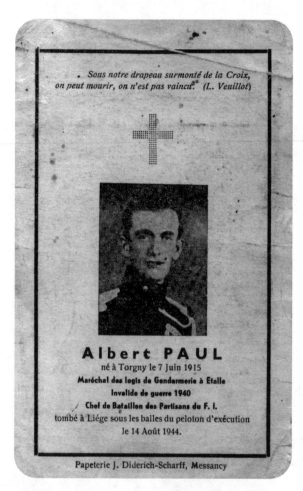

Sous notre drapeau surmonté de la Croix,
on peut mourir, on n'est pas vaincu. (L. Veuillot)

Albert PAUL
né à Torgny le 7 Juin 1915
Maréchal des logis de Gendarmerie à Etalle
Invalide de guerre 1940
Chef de Bataillon des Partisans du F. I.
tombé à Liége sous les balles du peloton d'exécution
le 14 Août 1944.

Papeterie J. Diderich-Scharff, Messancy

Albert Paul, Maréchal des logis de Gendarmerie, Etalle Belgium. Executed by
the German Gestapo at La Citadelle Saint Walburge, Liège Belgium 14 August
1944. Courtesy Paul family.

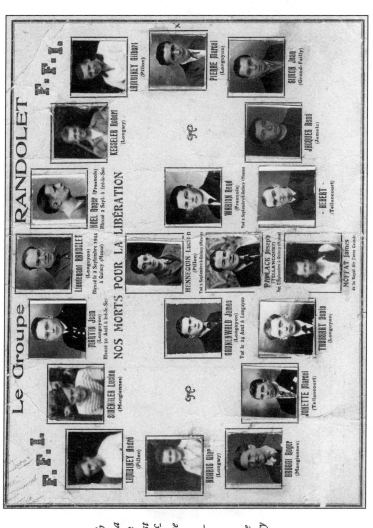

Le Groupe RANDOLET

F. F. I.

F. F. I.

NOS MORTS POUR LA LIBÉRATION

Jim Moffat fought with "Le Groupe Randolet," a French Maquis unit in northeast France, August - September 1944. Moffat is centre bottom. The four Maquis killed in action—James Grunenwald, Lucien Hennequin, René Warion and Joseph Pawlack are pictured centre. Courtesy Randolet Group.

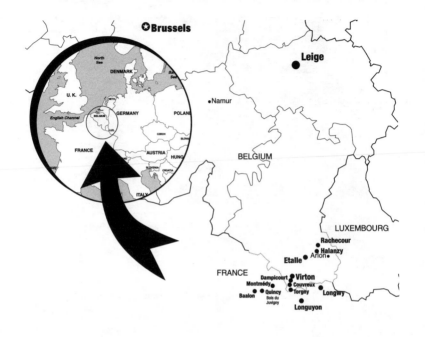

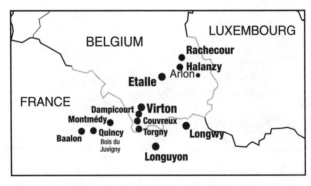

Map of southern tip of Belgium - north east tip of France. Jim Moffat hid from the Germans here. He was helped by the Belgian Resistance from Etalle to the Virton-Torgny area. He fought with the French Maquis around Iré-le-Sec to Juvigny, to the battle at Quincy.

Forty-four years after jumping out an upstairs window fleeing from the Germans, Jim Moffat embraces Cécile Macé (formerly Cécile Paul) who had hidden Moffat and another Allied airman in her home in 1944. They were reunited in May 1988.

The town of D'Aubange Belgium, which includes Halanzy and Rachecourt, erected a monument to the crews of the RCAF Halifax and RAF Lancaster which crashed the night of March 30-31, 1944. Jim Moffat, left, spoke at the unveiling in Rachecourt on March 31, 1990. Arsène Martin initiated the monument.

CHAPTER NINE

DESIRÉ PAUL WAS OLDER THAN ALBERT, more of Vital's age, in his late thirties or early forties. I was too young to tell. He was short, about five foot five. His nose hooked over a small, almost cherubic face. His light, sandy hair swept up in a small pompadour. Not at all like his cousins Vital and Albert. He was dressed in the light green uniform of the Belgian forestry service. We set a slow pace as we headed out of the sheep field. I was still wearing soft slippers, no socks. I had walked all the previous day and night to get to wherever it was that I was. I had apparently crossed the French border and was about fifteen miles into France. Now Desiré and I walked all day back into Belgium.

Albert Paul had been taken by the Germans. Vital was in close touch with the resistance movement and had warned Desiré to keep a watch out for me. I wasn't quite sure if the young shepherd had reported me to the resistance network or just how I'd been located. But it was a sign of their persistent battle against the occupation that they never gave up on me, even with their worries over Albert. Or maybe it was because of their worries over Albert that they determined to help me, as a way of showing their determination. And now I was one of their own. We talked very little and kept a watch out for signs of anyone. I thought as I walked along how brave these people were to make contact with me when they knew the Germans were on the look out for me.

Desiré was taking me to the Paul family's hometown. Torgny. This village of about 300 people lies just south of Virton. It sits right at the border with France. We kept to the road and walked most of the day. We entered the village from a hill road on the south. It snuggled in the valley, surrounded by steep hills of pasture and forest. Desiré's home was on the edge of the village, a one-storey, two-bedroom cottage. We went down the last hill directly to the cottage. Once again I was taken into the Paul family. Madame Paul immediately cooked a meal for me. A little girl, a replica of her father except that she was blonde, stared at me, wide-eyed and silent. She was about three. Another girl, a little older, was quite sickly. I thought only of my own hunger and thirst. Once I'd eaten and had some coffee we had to consider the position.

Desiré said, "You can't stay here. I know a place for you." Darkness had crept over the village while I ate so that I couldn't really get a good look at my surroundings. I followed Desiré along the road to an old church. It was a two hundred year old brick building, covered with stucco, set back up the hill on the outskirts of the village road. Only a large doorway and the plain square bell tower broke the facade. The bell tower topped the front of the building with a modest peak. The windows were boarded up. A long, low, brick annex ran out at the back. This was L'Hermitage, the hermitage, once a church but now a closed down museum. It was to be my home. Desiré removed the boarding from one of the low side windows at the back, and we crawled into the side of the church and up into the rafters. Even after the long walk Desiré was as nimble as a monkey climbing into the rafters. I followed him onto the ridge pole and crawled to the end of that. This brought us to the front of the church, into the uppermost part at the bell tower. I stood up and looked around in wonder.

We were in a little room, about ten feet by ten feet. The windows here were boarded up as well but one of them was easily removed. A little fireplace sat in one corner. It was covered with boarding. And on the floor there was a straw sack. A sack full of straw for me to sleep on. He said, "You stay here at night. In the day time you will go into the forest. I'll bring you some food in the forest, every day." He left me there, making his exit carefully over the rafters and back down to slip out the side of the building. I was ready for a good night's sleep. My stomach was full and I was with friends again. I wasn't on my way to Switzerland, or anywhere for that matter, but I curled up on the sack quite content with my fate at the moment.

I awoke the next morning ready to begin this new pattern in my life. Desiré had told me where to meet him in the woods. I left the church early and walked up a small roadway leading from the main highway that passed through the village, up the hill and into the edge of the forest. I waited for Desiré just inside the cover of the woods. I was beginning to feel really quite at home in the woods after these past few days. It was now past mid-May and the day was warm. I walked up and down listening to the birds and absorbing the sense of the forest. I hadn't long to wait before Desiré appeared.

He had brought me the inevitable bacon grease sandwich, which I ate thankfully, and a drink of water. And then came the news. *"Les sales Boches, ils ont capture Albert,"* he said. "They have taken Albert. Albert is a prisoner. They have taken him to the prison in Arlon. Both Albert and the English airman were captured. We don't know what is happening, or how they are." Then he told me what little he knew of what happened after I had jumped out of the upstairs window as the Germans rushed Albert's home in Etalle. The Gestapo already had Albert, and held him right at the front door. Bill Jones had been shot in the leg as he raced across the field. The Gestapo dragged him to the front of the house as well. I learned many years later that they told Jones "the other guy," meaning me, was lying dead in the field. Albert and Bill Jones were taken to the German prison at Arlon. Vital had learned this much and passed it along to Desiré. No one had any further news of the prisoners.

Desiré was not as worldly as his cousins. Vital was in direct contact with the allies in London. He was a vital part of the resistance movement. Albert Paul was a striking force, a big, joking personality who had been away to war before Belgium was occupied and then had played a key role in the *Maquis*. Desiré lived a simpler life. The capture of his cousin was a blow to him.

Desiré Paul was the local forester. He patrolled the area to make sure the laws of the forest were obeyed and of course this gave him quite a bit of freedom of movement. His hobby was collecting beetles. He did this for the museum in Virton, about ten miles away. "Would you like to come and help me?" he asked one day. I jumped at the chance. Desiré would bring a little bottle with some ether in it. He and I would go out into the forest, looking under leaves. Anything interesting, in other words beetles of all shapes and sizes, we'd pop into the bottle. We'd collect all kinds of them. I didn't know anything about it, but Desiré knew many of the names and species and would classify them. He warned me, "There's one beetle that will spit and it's sort of poisonous. The spit can hurt your eyes. Be careful." Desiré had small boxes about four by five inches with foam in the bottom and glass on top. He would take the beetles out of the ether bottle, stick pins in them, and put them on the foam with the glass over. We'd spend hours doing this a couple of times a week. He would have about ten or fifteen boxes ready for the museum. It was an education for me and highly interesting.

A couple of times a week Edmond-Pierre Fouss, creator and curator of the *Musée Gaumais* in Virton, would come out to the Paul home. Fouss was a conservationist who had established a museum dedicated to *La Gaume*. Virton is at Belgium's southernmost tip, at the heart of *La Gaume*, an area which he had come to love. He had dedicated his life to recording the nature, the folklore, the language and archaeology of *La Gaume*. He established the *Musée Gaumais* in an ancient convent of *Recollets* in Virton, just before the war, to preserve the regional heritage.

It was Fouss also who was interested in the history of my new home, L'Hermitage de Notre-Dame de Luxembourg. The chapel had been guarded by a hermit as early as 1730. It had fallen into ruin after that for about 100 years. At that time another hermit rehabilitated it, and made himself a cell for living, and a special place for his tomb. He even created a couple of towers. When he died in 1875 he was buried in the cemetery in Torgny instead of the tomb he'd made. By the time I'd entered the scene the towers had fallen into ruin, the chapel had been hit by several shells early in the war and was closed to the public. This was perfect for my snug hideaway.

Fouss would come out to pick up the boxes of beetles that we had collected. He was a stocky man about fifty years old and very agile. Sometimes he would bring a butterfly net. It was like a cartoon. I never thought I would ever see someone dashing across a field with a net, chasing butterflies. But Fouss would often do just that. One day when he came for his visit he brought me the London Illustrated News from 1918. The year he'd been at Oxford learning English. He talked of those days and of the world of bugs. I drank it in.

The Germans were moving at night now. The pressure from the allies was greater every day. From my little window in the belfry I would occasionally see a truck or car roll through the village but this was a country road and there was not a great amount of traffic. One day I was in the forest waiting for Desiré. He always brought me one meal a day. I looked up to see him running toward me. I could tell he was excited. I was a little apprehensive because it could mean the Germans were raiding the village. Then he was calling to me *"Le débarquement! Le débarquement!"* D-Day. The landing at Normandy. It was June 6, 1944. It was what everyone was waiting for, talked about, prayed for. He was ecstatic and I was in heaven. In a week or so I would be liberated. I was sure of that. About a week later he came with more news. This time about the German buzz bombs. "Airplanes. Pilotless airplanes. Flying. Bombing London." I thought, 'The Germans must have launched some secret weapon. We could lose the war after all.'

One day I watched American bombers, Flying Fortresses and Liberators, flying over in formation. The sunlight glinting off their wings. A daylight raid on Berlin. A few hours later I spotted them on their way back, a number of holes in the formation, missing aircraft. I yearned to be up there. About the same time I heard a plane in the valley. A German *Focke-wulf* 190, flying close to the tree tops, ignoring the Americans. He was probably heading home. An enemy aircraft, but a beautiful sight, dipping over hills and into valleys below me.

Most of the time I was alone in the woods, but I enjoyed that. Desiré had given me a book *"Quel Donc Est Cette Ouiseau?"* What is this bird? I learned all the birds and the trees. Many of them I learned in French when I didn't even know them in English. I was trying to improve my French every day. I would help Desiré with his work a couple of times a week, the rest of the time I was on my own. I was feeling very hopeful again.

For two or three weeks we kept to this routine, all the time waiting for liberation. But then I began to itch. At first I thought it was just the sleeping on a sack of straw. During the day I was comfortable enough, but at night it was hell when my body got warm in the bed. Toward the end of June I went for three or four days without sleep. I tossed and turned and walked the floor all night. It would take me half an hour to get my pants down. They would be stuck to my rear. I had boils and scabies all over me. Scabies are little mites that burrow under the skin and lay eggs. They cause itching which is most intense at night. I had probably picked them up from the pants I had been given by the woodsman a few weeks earlier. Between them and the boils I was bleeding and in pretty bad shape. I told Desiré, "I need a doctor. I need a doctor badly."

We knew it was dangerous but that night he took me to his home. It was a five minute walk from L' Hermitage down the hill to the village. His wife was there, Henriette Paul. She was a husky, dark-haired woman, bigger in build than Desiré.

Very pleasant looking, but her eyes were determined. She obviously ruled the roost and didn't like the idea of dealing with this unless she had to. It was to be her decision whether or not we got a doctor. "Down the pantaloon," she commanded. "No way. No way," I answered, quite startled by the idea. Eventually she convinced me that if I wanted a doctor I'd better let her look at the worst of me. I dropped my trousers and she gasped, "Oh *mon Dieu*. Tonight you stay here." The next morning Desiré went on his forestry rounds as usual and I stayed in the house.

About mid-morning Madame Paul, Henriette, answered a knock at the door. There was the quiet rumbling of talk. She came back to me and said, "A truck will come tomorrow. It will take you to a nice lady's home and you will stay there. They will take you to a doctor." Early the next morning a truck wheezed its way up to the front of the Paul's house. It was an old flat-bed truck with a big black thing hanging on the side of the cab. It was a relic. A charcoal burner which somehow made the gas. I climbed aboard and we wheezed our way to the next village, about 10 minutes away. A village called Dampicour. The mayor of Dampicour was Monsieur Adam. It was to his house they took me. And then what a surprise! His wife Madame Adam was an English woman.

"How are you," she welcomed me in her English tones. "By your accent I'd say you're from Yorkshire. I'm based in Yorkshire in the Royal Canadian Air Force. What is your home town?" I asked. "Oh," she said, "It's just a little town you've never heard of it. It's called Pontefract." "Oh my God, my mother's from Pontefract." And so we talked about my mother, and Madame Adam told me how she came to be in this little village in southern Belgium. She had been a nurse in the Belgian army in the first World War. She married a Belgian soldier and stayed in his country. And there she was in the midst of another war.

Monsieur Adam was the mayor of Dampicour, and he ran the local sawmill. Madame Adam told me that he was sympathetic to the German cause. She said, "I do my work in the resistance. We tell him if he doesn't like it and he does anything about it, we will burn down his sawmill. So he keeps quiet." She may have been joking but I don't think so. They had two children. I didn't see the son, but the daughter was a beauty. She was 18 years old. "It is a terrible war," said Madame Adam. "My son and my daughter, it is the time of life when they should socialize and they can't. It's terrible for them."

After supper she said, "Of course you'll want a bath." The first in two months. There I was clean and in a nice warm bed and I was scratching five times as much. The next morning when I arose there was blood all over the bed sheets. She said, "Oh, you really need a doctor. The truck will be coming this morning."

The same truck showed up and we wheezed away into the forest. After a bit it slowed down and there were three young men in their late teens with guns, waiting for me. All I could think of was, "Where's the doctor?' They urged me to go along, and we walked about a mile further into the woods. The two of them started whistling. Whistling a tune. Then I heard someone whistling the same tune in answer, just a short distance away. I didn't see anyone, but we had passed through some kind of security gateway. As we neared the camp I saw a tall, Slavic looking fellow with short blond hair come out. He was whistling, marching along, holding a gun on a German soldier. My companion said, "He's going for his final walk." And then there we were. This really was the underground. An underground dugout. A huge hideout dug out of the hillside. The forest was dark and damp under the huge beech and maple trees. The outside was camouflaged with trees. Blankets were hung at the doorway.

The resistance groups, the *Maquis,* were very active in Luxembourg province of Belgium. There were the mountains and the woods of the Ardenne, and they had taken over the old iron mines in the Halanzy and Musson areas which had been shut down during the war. Many resistance units hid out in the mines around Halanzy. The Germans didn't like the dangers posed by the roof racks and avoided the mines. These *Maquis* units were made up of mostly young men, many Belgian soldiers who had escaped the Germans. Many were French and Russian soldiers hiding out. They lived as best they could and did what damage they could.

The records of their clandestine actions show that they worked persistently, and under dangerous conditions, to sabotage the occupation forces. A picture of *"Le Maquis de Musson"* shows young determined men, defiantly holding a unit flag, and some pointing their guns at the camera. By 1944 the Halanzy resistance members were stepping up their activities, putting *"fer de poussierre",* iron dust, in the oil boxes of rail cars, cutting telephone and hydro wires. C. Buysse wrote in the *Maquis* journal that they would force pieces of sharply filed iron into the pavement on the roadways to cut the tires of German truck convoys. At one point the unit decided to hit the German provisions train running through Halanzy. After watching for three nights they determined the exact timing. Nine of the men worked to lift the tracks. Then at 10:25 P.M right on time, the train came rushing along at sixty kilometres an hour. The armed men flagged it down but the engineer refused to stop and the train hit the lifted track. It was derailed, the two locomotives damaged, and more importantly traffic was held up for thirty-six hours.

Of course, the Germans took their reprisals, often on the villagers, sometimes violent sometimes not. Eight days after this incident the Germans came to the village, took eighteen bicycles and all the hidden T.S.F., radios, they could find. The summary of work by the *Maquis* section at Athus shows the kind of serious damage and psychological irritation the units accomplished. It gave them great satisfaction to pass around an underground journal, and hang the forbidden Belgian flag on public buildings whenever there was a national occasion. They manufactured identity and work cards. They repatriated escaped Belgian prisoners of war who were returning home under cover, and helped Allied airmen. They tracked down the Gestapo whenever possible, and when the time came they revealed the collaborators to the liberating armies.

The meticulous records, for instance by M. Boterberge of the *Maquis de Musson*, show the trauma and the desperation felt by the death of a comrade in the close-knit group as when Pierre Luttgens died in the fight to liberate Athus. But in the same paragraph he tells of the American liberation of 9 September 1944. Members of the *Maquis* climbed aboard the American tanks to liberate Messancy.

I had heard of the resistance, just bits and pieces on the base in England, and of course while we lived with Albert Paul, but I hadn't heard of anyone living under ground. The two men led me inside. The cave or dugout was about thirty feet deep and maybe fifteen feet wide. The ten foot ceiling was braced by timbers. Fairly roomy but there were about twenty men there. All with guns, various types of rifles and pistols. There were introductions all around. First names only. No one questioned my identity. Of course I had identification as the Belgian Charles Lebrun, but I had none as Flying Officer James Moffat in the R.C.A.F. There were two Algerians from the French Army, two Russians who had escaped from the Germans, one guy from Luxembourg, and all the rest were Belgians. A tall, blond fellow with a Vandyke beard appeared to be the leader. He was Flemish, from the north. I immediately asked if any one could speak English. Just my luck, nobody could.

There were bunks, just carved out of the dirt, about two feet high all along the sides. Blankets were laid on them. I was assigned a bunk. It was damp, and cold. There was no fire. The cooking fire was outside. Later when we had all gone to bed I heard the Algerians and the Russians speaking broken English. I called out, "Why don't you speak to me in English?" They didn't answer. Finally one of the Belgians explained in French that they were speaking broken German. To me it had sounded like broken English, but at least it was a way to communicate. The next day I was told I'd have yet another wait for the doctor. He was expected in the next few days. Meanwhile I was to take my turn at guard duty. The *Maquis* leader explained to me that this unit was not doing any fighting. They were just staying in hiding. Often moving their encampment. But right now they were staying put.

I was assigned guard duty with one of the Russians, Nikolai Sapranov. Nikolai didn't speak any French or English, the only two languages I knew, but he did speak the broken German. We spent a lot of time together. We'd go out about half a mile toward the edge of the woods and watch for the Germans. And we'd try to communicate. We'd get down on our knees and draw pictures. Nikolai was about my height but heavier, about 180-pounds. Blond hair topped a round head. He was like a big kid. He laughed a lot and didn't seem to take anything seriously. Often quite ridiculous. Nikolai taught me a Russian song, a few phrases in Russian and of course, a few swear words and some German. His German was fairly good, he'd had lots of practice. This was his story as far as I could make it out. He was a bomber pilot from Moscow, shot down on a mission over Berlin. The other Russian in camp was Yenka or Jenka, an artillery officer who'd been captured in battle. They were a strange duo since Yenka was short and stocky, also blond but with a wide, intelligent face. The two had met while in a prisoner of war camp in Germany. They had escaped together. In fact, they had escaped twice before. This was the third time. Nikolai said, "We got to the Swiss border, two times. Two times we were captured. Now we think we can get there again and get into Switzerland." I said, "Whenever you decide to go I want to go with you. I don't want to stay here." One of the Algerians in camp, Aidi Mohamad, was also friendly toward me. He helped me to communicate with the Russians as well.

It was about a week later that the doctor came. We could hear his motorcycle coming for miles away. He left it near the roadway and walked in. He checked me over and decided to give me an injection. He got out a big, old-fashioned needle and shot it into my arm. I passed out, crumpled to the ground. I don't know how long I was out but when I came to the doctor was talking to the resistance leader. "You'd better get him to some place where he can get some good food. He's suffering malnutrition. He has scabies and a number of other things wrong with him." And so once again I waited for treatment. One day a priest came and there was an outdoor church service for the Roman Catholics. Nikolai and I stood guard duty. Two days later one of the men said, "You're coming with me. We're going to take you to a home where you can stay. They'll give you white bread, lots of greens, lots of lettuce and good food." I was thankful there was no more talk of medical treatment. So we walked, slowly, to the little town of Couvreux, about five or six kilometres away. By this time I wasn't able to walk very fast. We came to the home of Madame Germaine Autphenne.Madame Autphenne was tall, upright, with her hair brushed modestly back from a kind, open face. She had the clothes and bearing of an old-fashioned school teacher, which is what she was. She had two little girls. Her husband was a major in the Belgian army. A hero. Earlier in the war his little anti-tank unit of thirty men had held up a whole German division for two days. But now he was paying the price for his heroism. Major Autphenne had been captured and was in a German prison camp in Hamburg.

Madame Autphenne welcomed me into her home and gave me fresh biscuits with butter and honey. Her job with the resistance was to help look after those who became ill, especially if they just needed some good food to build them up. She had a flourishing garden with lots of greens, and six box beehives sitting at the bottom. Again the instructions were that I couldn't leave the house. Her brother Guy was living there also. Guy Giot was in the *Maquis* but was home recovering from an accident. I knew him only as "Emile," his resistance name at the time. He had had the inside of his hand blown out. The Allies were dropping explosives to the resistance. The little Teller mines were dropped in two pieces, the explosive and the detonator. The detonator was heavily smeared in vaseline. He had been wiping the vaseline off and must have accidentally touched the trigger. When he heard the telltale "pssstt" he threw it, but it exploded in his hand.

Chapter Ten

The tiny village of Couvreux sits at the French border, in the tail of the Ardennes south west of Virton. Madame Autphene had a comfortable home right in the village, with a large garden at the back. It was really a home attached to the school. I shared a room with Emile. Emile was a tall, slim fellow with broad shoulders. His fair hair curled round a wide face in a careless manner. Of course, he was no stranger to his sister's home and felt perfectly at ease. But the restrictions of hiding in the house, and a bandaged hand, were making him restless. He had spent months fighting in the resistance. He was looking for action. My arrival acted as a catalyst to prompt that action.

One night just after my arrival Madame Autphene was out at a meeting. Emile found the key to the liquor cabinet and took out the brandy. He fiddled about with the old radio in the front room and found the BBC. Emile was generous, and the two of us sat back drinking brandy, enjoying second and thirds. This was a relaxing evening after all my troubles. But trouble was on its way home in the guise of Germaine Autphene. She was a brisk, determined woman, much like my own mother. A very assured, self-contained woman who had had to make a life for herself and two children amid the hardships of the German occupation. And she was putting all that on the line for us. She marched into the room, switched off the radio and gave her brother an earful. No one was allowed to listen to the BBC. We did listen most nights but at a very low volume. If we were reported to the Germans, or if they heard it themselves, they would be pounding on the door. She was furious with us.

I was now eating and sleeping well but still quite weak. It was July and the weather was fine. Madame Autphene and the girls were next door at school. One child was old enough to go to school, the other she took along with her. In this way she was able to make a living. On the third day Emile said, "Let's go swimming." I said, "O.K but I don't have any swimming trunks." With a wide grin and a toss of those blond curls he said, "I'll fix that." He rummaged around his sister's wardrobes and came up with a pair of her bloomers. "These are for you," he said with a laugh and off we went.

The Semois River is a natural border between Belgium and France, curving now into one country and now into the other. It winds its way through Virton and touches the little villages as it heads south east. We eased our way along the riverbank, following the farmland, staying by the cover of bushes when we could. It was a hot day and we swam for an hour or so before heading home.

The success of this venture spurred Emile to try again. A few days later he threw out this lure. "Why don't we go fishing?" 'Well,' I thought, "at least this won't involve wearing bloomers.' He had a couple of eight foot bamboo poles, fishing line and hooks. But there was a problem. "We can't fish in Belgium because you have to have a license. I can't get a license because I ran way from a work camp in Germany. We'll walk over into France where we won't need a license." What irony. In the midst of war we were worrying about a simple fishing license. But it made sense to avoid any trouble.

Emile said that it was only about a mile and I felt fit enough for that kind of exercise. We crossed a footbridge over the Semois River to the village of Ecouviez, France. It was a pretty little village with about 20 houses scattered around the river. One of these was a bakery and tavern. We propped our fishing rods against the wall, and went in. The aroma of fresh bread and beer circled our heads. We bought a bun and a pint of beer. We picked up our rods and strolled down the river path for a mile or so out into the country. The sun shone on my face as I sat by the river, watching my line through half closed eyelids, soaking up the warmth. Fluffy clouds were drifting slowly overhead. Peace. Then I spotted someone in uniform. He was dressed in dark navy or black with a pill box hat. "A French policeman," I whispered. He was actually a customs officer for the France - Belgium border. He strolled up to us and started talking to Emile about fishing. Emile answered quite easily. Then the officer turned to me. My accent wasn't trustworthy. I just smiled and answered, "Fine. I agree."

Nobody mentioned the war. Nobody mentioned the Germans. We were in France. It was difficult to know who would be sympathetic to the resistance and who would be collaborators. Normally there would be no young men around. Most would be working in Germany or hiding with the resistance.

We were obviously young men. This put us on the spot. As soon as he left Emile said, "We'd better go home."

We put our fishing poles over our shoulder and walked back into Ecouviez. We were walking down the middle of the dirt road that was the village street when we heard a "beep beep" behind us. We stepped to the side. There came an open touring car with two members of the *"Organization Todt"* in the front seat. This was an organization started by a German engineer and general called Fritz Todt. When Hitler came to power he put Todt in charge of transportation and construction of *autoroutes*. Todt was soon named minister of armaments and munitions. He gave his name to a paramilitary organization which used workers from occupied countries to build the Atlantic wall and other military buildings for the German army throughout occupied Europe. Todt built the Siegfried line. He erected gigantic monuments to the glory of nazism in Nuremburg. And a stadium to hold 500,000 spectators. The *"Todt"* members all wore tan coloured uniforms. Sitting in the back seat of this touring car were a couple of real German officers. As they drove by I worried, 'Why are we risking our lives? We'd better get the hell out of here.' But when we reached the bakery Emile said, "We'll have one more beer, then we'll go home." That same night Germaine found out we had been fishing. "Are you stupid. I am hiding you two. I am trying to protect you. I am risking my life and the lives of my children, and you do this." Emile made his apologies. I just kept quiet. I had thought that it was stupid from the first but I thought he knew what he was doing, and I had really wanted the walk.

After I had been with the Autphenes for a couple of weeks, Germaine came to me. "Are you afraid of bees?" she asked. "Would you help me take the honey out of the beehives?" I said, "I've never done it before but I'm willing to give it a try." Germaine looked at me. "I get stung every time," she said. Now my father was a man who knew a little bit about everything. Or at least he thought he did. "My father told me that if you're not scared of them the bees won't sting you. When you're scared you emit fear. The bees smell it and it drives them crazy." "Ah," she said, "but I get stung anyway. I'll do the smoke and you do the taking out of the honey trays." I knew she was afraid although she pretended not to be. We put on hats, nets and gloves and walked down the garden to the beehives. Germaine filled the bellows with smoke from the charcoal burner.

I bravely lifted off the lid of the first hive. Hundreds of little yellow bees buzzed like angry wasps at a picnic. They swirled round the trays in the boxed hive. She lifted the bellows which were like those used to encourage fires to burn, and started the smoke belching. I had a little whisk broom. I pulled out the first tray, brushed away the cluster of buzzing bees, and put the tray aside. I managed to get all the four trays out of each of the hives, inserting new ones in their places. All the time Germaine kept up the belching smoke to chase the bees from their homes. I thought, 'This is a piece of cake.' I could hear her. "Ouch, Ouch." Nothing was touching me. It took us about an hour to get all the honey out and put everything back in place because I was going so carefully. Not so bad a job for a first time. Then I looked at my arms. A wave of sickness came over me. A three inch layer of bees spread over both my arms. And the bees were crawling, crawling. 'Don't panic, don't panic,' I said to myself. I slowly backed away from the area, brushing gently at the bees with the whisk. They headed peacefully back to their hives. Germaine had been stung seven times. I hadn't been stung at all. Back in the kitchen she baked fresh white biscuits and we ate them warm, dripping with honey.

I expected to stay in Couvreux two or three weeks. I had to eat well, get rid of the scabies and gain some strength. I had some fresh trousers and I was bathing as often as possible. Emile's girl friend and her mother came by one day and we all had our picture taken, me in borrowed shirt and tie. It was all very normal, although it could certainly be dangerous to have these pictures.

But soon I would go back to the *Maquis* camp. I thought, 'If I go back there and get sick again I'll surely die there. I'm putting my money on the Russians. They've made it to the Swiss border in the past. Sure, they were captured. They've made mistakes. Now they have a good chance of getting across the border. Or at least they think they do. And that's what I think as well. I'll get better. I'll be able to walk. And I'll join the Russians on the trek to Switzerland.'

One of my main worries was that I had no identification. Nothing to say that I was Flying Officer James Moffat. If I was shot by the Germans, or died in any way, no one would know who I really was. My mother would never know. I was still carrying the identification as a Belgian worker, Charles Lebrun. This was preying on my mind. So one night I talked to Germaine. "Could you make me something with my name on it?" I asked. And she did. She sewed a little purse for my money. I marked my name, rank and birth date in it with indelible pencil.

Then it was the day. Two men came to take me back to the *Maquis* camp in the woods. I said goodbye to Madame Autphene. Another goodbye to someone who had saved my life. A someone who had risked her life to save mine. I would never forget her.

We walked back to the camp in the *Bois de Lahage* about seven kilometres north of Dampicour. We were no longer at the dugout, but just camping out in the rough, sleeping on the ground. I was certainly feeling stronger, and determined to make a break for it. I was also determined to have a bath every three or four days to make sure I kept clean, in good condition and no more scabies. When I told Nikolai he said, "We want a bath too. We'll help." The Belgian fellows could go home and clean up, have a meal and come back to the woods. We couldn't. We went to the creek nearby, well below where we took the drinking water from, and dug a hole in the creek bed about two feet deep. It was nice soft sand and not too difficult. We took off our clothes and jumped in. A hot summer day but the water was ice cold. We had no soap but scrubbed ourselves with sand. I still had the same shirt that I had originally been given in Etalle, the pants I had been given by the Autphenes, and the boots given to me by the *Maquis*. They had also given me a razor and razor blade. And showed me how to sharpen the razor so that it would last for weeks. I would take a glass of water, sit down on the grassy knoll and move the razor blade back and forth for nearly an hour until it was sharp again.

I hadn't been on any raids with the Belgians but one day two of the men were to pay a visit to a nearby village. They asked if I'd like to go along. We went to a small grocery store staffed by a teenage girl. The men asked for her father by name. She said he was away for the day. We left and one of the men said he was lucky. I'm not sure if they were ready to shoot him as a collaborator, or just because he wouldn't give us any food.

It was about this time that the *Maquis* leader decided to augment our meagre rations with a bit of exotic fare. We would shoot *un sanglier sauvage*. We were going wild boar hunting! First they explained the intricacies of preparing the bullets. The wild boar were so strong that when shot they could run for five or six kilometres before falling dead. So the trick was to cut a cross in the lead of the bullets and put pieces of string in the cross. This would cause the bullets to explode when they struck the animal. For two or three nights a few of us sat in the moonlight at the edge of someone's potato field. Waiting for a wild boar to come digging his favourite food, potatoes. Finally on the third night there he was. He was quickly shot and carried back to camp. We built a camp fire and cooked the boar over it. The meat was strong. Black and strong. It reminded me of a beaver we had eaten for Christmas on the farm one year. And it hit my system hard, starting up the boils on my body once again.

My guard duty with Nikolai had resumed. I had left my gun at the camp while I was at the Autphenes but now had it back. After about a week I got up courage to talk to the Russians. "I think we should get out of here. I'm concerned about what's happening." The two Russians were concerned as well. This *Maquis* unit had been told by the Allies to lie low. Not to do any sabotage or fighting. When the time came the Allies would parachute in some arms, and the fighting would begin. But now the waiting. What concerned us was that every once in a while four or five of the men would go into a town hunting for food. They would force the people to give them food and money. I said to Nikolai, "If they continue to do this someone's going to tell the Germans and we'll be in the bag." I was learning to communicate in German. It was difficult but we got by. "I want to go but I don't think they'll let us go. They worry that if we get caught we might talk." I outlined a plan. Both Russians agreed. They were eager to go as well. "I will go for a pail of water. You go for wood." *"Aah da,"* they said. The group was always looking for volunteers so our plan worked easily. About noon the next day the Russians approached a couple of men in the camp. "We will look for wood," and off they went. I said, "I'll get the water." There were no questions asked and off I went. We met in the woods and started to run.

We ran all that day. We just headed south toward France and ran. We ran through the wooded areas. We ran through fields. We would stop for a short rest to catch our breath then run again. Actually after the first few hours, when we were taking a short rest, I decided to get rid of my Belgian identification papers. The papers I had been given in Etalle while staying with Albert Paul. I hated to do it but it was just too dangerous to keep them. If the Germans caught me with false papers, using the name Charles Lebrun, disguised as a Belgian civilian, I knew I would likely be shot as a spy. I tore them up and buried them in the ground where we were resting.

We stayed to the fields and forests and saw not even a village. The second day was really hard. Yenka had been wounded earlier on in the war and limped. This slowed us down. It was difficult keeping up to Nikolai who went like the wind. We stuck to the forest, with only a mile or two of open space every now and then. There were farms, but we kept away from them. Again we slept just at the edge, under a canopy of beech and maples. The days were hot and dry and so were we. We had crossed only one little stream and all three of us were hot and thirsty. And hungry. We'd had nothing to eat all this time. We were well down into France now. We decided to try walking at night on a road that was heading in our direction, south and little bit east. Our magnet was drawing us to Switzerland, or so we thought.

Daybreak on the third day caught us in flat country with farms, and a village in the distance. A light, drizzly rain touched our faces. The first rain in weeks. We spotted a few trees and some bushes and headed across the field toward them. We found ourselves out in a rolling field, facing a wide river. There was no bridge, no boat and no woods for cover. I said, "We'd better find a place to sleep and lay up for the day." The landscape offered just those few trees, and a clump of bushes by the river. The ground around this was soggy with about an inch of water laying on it. It was the only hiding spot in sight so all three of us lay in the clump of bushes, in the water, hanging on to each other for warmth. We woke up hungry. We hadn't eaten for three days.

Well we had eaten but it had not been a good thing. The day before we had stopped in a farmer's field. It was a field full of leafy stuff, maybe an exotic lettuce. It had a cabbagey taste. We ate a bit of it and all three of us were sick. It was a field of tobacco plants. We'd been hit with nicotine poisoning. This was our third day on the run. As soon as we awoke, about noon, we headed up river looking for a way to cross, a boat or bridge. We didn't want to get too close to the village since there was no forest cover nearby. A way over on the other side of the field we saw a man working. Alone. We decided to chance it. We walked over. He was dressed all in black. A short, elderly Italian hoeing potatoes in the field. He spoke reasonably good French. "We are on our way to Switzerland," I said. "We haven't eaten in three days." He was immediately sympathetic. "I'll give you food," he said. He handed us one raw egg. We punched a hole in one end. We passed that egg around three times,

sucking the raw egg out of that tiny hole. Not one of us
wanted to take more than his share. The old Italian broke
up his one sandwich into three pieces and we shared that.
He had tea in a wine bottle. We drank that. The old fellow
got more and more excited at this adventure. He was speaking French but as his excitement increased he gradually
switched to Italian and I couldn't understand a word.

"I know someone who can help you," he said, again in
French. "I'll go get someone." He seemed friendly enough
but we decided to take no more chances. As soon as he left
we ran back about 400 feet. There was a small quarry at the
edge of the field. We crouched down behind some bushes
there. If he brought back a contingent of Germans we
would be ready to run. If he came back with just one person we would see what developed. Maybe an hour passed.
He came back with one person.

CHAPTER ELEVEN

THE TWO MEN WALKED ACROSS THE FIELD toward the spot where we'd met the little Italian. The farmer was hurrying, gesticulating and talking all the way. The other man was taller, quieter, and fairly well-dressed. His forehead reached far back to a receding hairline at the temples. The dark, sleek hair was combed straight back. A long, thin nose dominated his thin face. We came out of our hiding place and walked forward to meet them. *"Je suis Louis Paul,"* he said. *"Je suis un Maquisard."* I was thunderstruck. Another member of the Paul family helping me. But as it turned out he was no relation, had no connection. He was French and an active member of the resistance. He said that he would help get me back to England. Louis Paul spoke fluent German. He explained to the Russians that he would take them to a Polish underground camp. This was good news all round. Once again I had a surge of optimism. Once more I was on my way back to England.

We thanked our Italian friend and followed Louis Paul out to the roadway. There sat a small truck with a driver. We were near the village of Martincourt on the River Meuse. Instead of going south east toward Switzerland, for the past three days we had run about thirty kilometres directly west. Of course, a lot of that had been dodging around forests. Paul said, "Get in the back. You're just some foreign workers." We climbed into the back of the pickup and he hopped into the passenger seat. We drove along for about an hour on sandy, back country roads, not making much speed, the three of us rattling around in the back, barely speaking, just hoping. I was scared stiff someone would stop us. We stopped at the side of a road near a forest. He called to the Russians to jump down and, after a short consultation in German, they headed along a trail into the trees. There was a camp further back where Polish workers, who had escaped from German work camps, were hiding and the Russians would join them. I called goodbye to Nikolai and Yenka The last I saw of them they were heading into the woods. I was now alone in the truck bed. We continued on for a while, then suddenly stopped at the side of the road near another woods.

Louis Paul got out of the truck again and called to me to follow. We headed up a trail that led into the stand of tall maples and beech. *Le Bois de Chenois* near Baalon. The past weeks were dropping away as we walked. Now I would really be heading back. Louis Paul seemed to know what he was doing and his confidence flooded over me. I was moving forward, there was no looking back. We walked quickly and soon came to a little grove. Young men were spread about. They looked about seventeen to twenty-five years of age. They were leaning on trees, sitting, and walking about. Chatting. Some carrying guns. Some not. It looked very casual, and safe. And there was a comradeship. Louis Paul introduced me to his resistance group, and we all shook hands. He was obviously very proud of his little band of brigands.

He and I retraced our steps and got back into the truck. A fifteen minute drive over the bumpy, country road brought us to a little village. We drove to his home in Baalon. Actually I had no idea where I was at the time, but learned later that it was Baalon, France, about twenty kilometres west of Torgny, Belgium. I had not made much ground toward Switzerland, but had really been going in circles. I was still just south of Torgny. I met Madame Paul who immediately went to the kitchen to prepare some supper for us. Louis and I sat in the living room. He told me that he had been a lieutenant in the French army until the occupation. He was now heading up a unit of the *Maquis*. He talked of his resistance work. He was proud of their fight against the Germans and I think he wanted me to let London know just how much he was doing. This, of course, might help him get more weapons and possibly explosives from the Allies.

Then I heard yet another plan for my escape, and return to England. Paul outlined what steps would be taken. "We're going to get you false papers so that you will have identification again. Within a few days a plane will land nearby and you'll be flown back to England," he said. This was better than anything I'd heard so far. While I was on squadron I had heard about night cover flights by small planes, into occupied France, to pick up Allied agents and VIP evacuees. These were the British Lysander aircraft, affectionately known as "Lizzies." I just had time to think,

'Oh isn't this grand,' when the screaming began. *"Les Boches, les Boches."* Madame Paul came running into the room. *"Les Boches sont ici."*

Louis Paul reacted quickly. "There's a window out the back. Get out that back window and get lost. You don't know me. You never saw me. You never heard of me. And don't come back." I didn't answer. I ran to the back where there were French doors that opened on to a patio. I ran across the lawn and crawled through the thick hedge that bordered the property, with the idea of getting across the road. As I made my way through the hedge on my hands and knees I saw in front of me two boots and a rifle butt. I stopped right there, barely breathing. Once again I was hiding in a hedge. This time within inches of a German soldier standing guard. There was no movement. I tried to make myself comfortable without moving or breathing excessively. I didn't hear a sound and I had no idea what was happening. After a while a vehicle went by, and then another. That was all. There was no yelling, no shouting. Nothing. I could hear the cows and horses in a nearby field. The boots remained. And the rifle butt. After what seemed a couple of hours of this, a truck stopped on the roadside. I heard the German soldier talking, then some movement. Then the feet were gone, along with the soldier. The truck pulled away.

As soon as I felt sure that the coast was clear I dashed across the road. There I was faced with a wide open field. I decided to stay in some bushes just on the edge. There were a few cows and horses grazing. The horses were small, sway backed, with brown coats roughened by years of neglect. They smelled me, swung round as one, tails raised, and galloped to the other side. But the cows! First one, obviously the ring leader, snuffled loudly. She looked around, her large head swinging slowly, her doe-like, soft brown eyes staring. Then she headed my way, chewing her cud, head swaying, tail swishing at the flies, walking stolidly in her cow-like way. Her cow eyes stared stupidly toward the bush and by this time she was close enough that I smelled the manure caked on her back legs. She stopped a few feet away, uncertain. And behind her, strung out across the field, but already advancing, were her companions. A host of black and white pointer-cows showing just where I was hiding. I didn't dare call out but I thought it. 'Get out of here you stupid cows.' They kept it up. Staring toward me and snuffling. Luckily for me the Germans had gone. There was no one around to notice.

I sat in the bushes and tried to relax and keep calm. My adrenaline was running at high speed. I was planning what I should do next. No time to get discouraged. 'If I wait until about midnight I can be sure the Germans will be gone. I'll make my way back to that little band of *Maquis* in the woods. I'll have to follow the main street out onto the road, and find the trail that leads into the grove.' It seemed like a good idea, and my best plan now since I couldn't go back to Louis Paul's house. It had one drawback. I would have to go right through the village. I waited. The moon came up. Not a cloud softened its brightness. It's silver glow touched the countryside painting the trees and houses in black shadow, but spreading daylight along the roadway. I judged it to be about midnight and started down the main street, keeping an ear out for any motor vehicle sound that might bring the Germans back. I walked about five kilometres back down the road and sure enough I found the trail. In the moonlight I could see it plain as day. 'This is kind of stupid. A trail off the roadway that you can see like that. The enemy would certainly notice it.'

I hurried along the trail to the open glade. The moon

shone down on the camp, shimmering silver on the tree
tops, revealing the entire area and casting shadows on the
men sleeping there. Sleeping. There were no guards. Having
lived in *Maquis* camps already I knew that that was more
than stupid. It was dangerous. I didn't want to get shot by
startling someone so I called out, *"Bonjour, bonjour."* I
called my name. *"Je suis Charles Lebrun."* And again,
"Bonjour, bonjour." Nobody moved. I thought, 'Wait a
minute.' I walked closer into the camp and reached down to
touch one of the young men. His skin, glinting white in the
moonlight, was ice cold. Shot. All twenty of them. They'd
all been shot. I looked round. Most of them had had their
heads caved in. These laughing young men of the sunlight,
crushed. Shot and battered. I panicked. This was more than
I'd ever seen before or expected to see. I wasn't prepared. I
turned around to the path and ran. When I reached the road
I ran. I kept running. Just running and running. Not worrying about the moonlight, not worrying about possible
enemy traffic. I ran most of the night until I dropped. I
crawled into some bushes at the side of the road and fell
into an exhausted sleep.

I awoke to the sound of birds overhead. The late July
sun was already forecasting a hot summer day. I made my
way to the road, heavy with the sense of being alone again.
Exhausted, hungry and thirsty. I hadn't had time to eat the
meal being prepared by Madame Louis Paul. My only meal
in four days had been the Italian farmer's sandwich, and the
egg, shared with the Russians. I had no idea of the time but
the position of the sun told me that it was well into the
morning. The sun also told me the bad news. I had run the
wrong way. In my panic I had run north, heading back on
my route of the past few days. I was faced with retracing my

steps of the night before to get back on my way to Switzerland. This was still foremost in my mind.

Now that I was a little calmer I decided it would be foolish to travel on the roadway. I could see a power line overhead. I decided to follow it. I would travel during the day so that I could see where I was going. I would keep to the edge of the forest and if I saw anyone I could easily duck into the woods and wait. I thought, 'The Germans know there's someone around. They'll be on the lookout after yesterday's action. There will probably be patrols out scouting the area.' I left myself no time for despair. I was more experienced now and my focus was on Switzerland. I headed out, keeping a fairly slow but steady pace. I kept my eye on the roadway but no cars or trucks passed by. All was quiet and peaceful. A couple of times people could be seen walking along the road, but I ducked out of sight. I stayed away from the villages.

Then I saw him. I spotted him too late to duck into the cover of the forest. It would look too suspicious. I kept walking. I could see him quite clearly. He was in full khaki uniform. I couldn't tell if it was a Belgian soldier or a British officer. Definitely not German. We were both in an open field near the woods. He looked at me and I looked at him. We each turned the other way and kept going. It shook me, but I kept on as if nothing had happened. I wondered, 'What is he doing here? Is he connected in some way with the resistance? Should I have spoken to him? It's too late now. I'll never know if I did the right thing.'

I was hungry, and thirsty. My drive to reach Switzerland kept me going, but I had had nothing to eat. I walked all day and curled up in the woods that night. The second day I headed out again. I was keeping to the edge of the woods

when I heard voices. 'What's this.' I walked on, then edged
into the woods. I peered into a clearing not far into the tree
cover. *Deja vu.* The sun shone on rifles hanging from the
trees. Men dressed just in shorts and no shirts were tanning
themselves in the sunshine. Some with guns dangling from
their hands, some not. They were all talking excitedly in
French. 'They must have food and I need food, help of some
kind.' I strolled casually into the glade. *"Bonjour. Bonjour."*
Immediately there were three guns up my nose.

The chattering stopped. I was surrounded. They took
me prisoner. *"Tu travail pour les Boches.* You're working
for the Germans," they said. "You're our prisoner. We
won't waste a bullet on you we'll just hang you from a
tree." That frightened me. *"Je* suis *Canadien. Aviateur, aviateur,"* I kept repeating. "We don't know about that. Someone will come to see you in a few days." An armed guard
was assigned to me, day and night.

I had been foolish enough to think that joining this
happy group would mean a meal for me. They fed me all
right but it was meagre fare. They were living on their version of *blanc mange.* They made it with flour and water.
They had no milk. No salt. No gelatin. It was like eating
cooked dough. But I was hungry and I ate it gladly.

There were eighteen men in camp, I made the nineteenth.
Not that I had been accepted as such yet. They were mostly
in their early twenties. The camp in *Le Foret de Woevre* was
in a pleasant glade of soft grasses and much like the other I
had lived in. We slept on the ground and lived among the
trees. It was as simple as that. It was similar to the Belgian
camp. There were no sleeping bags, no blankets even. Of
course it was summer and the weather was good. At night
we just put on all our clothes and lay on the grass, with guns

close beside us. They were getting more and more friendly but never let up their guard with me. The *Maquis* leader was Lucien Sibénaler. He was a tall, slim fellow with dark, intense eyes. His face was clean cut with a determined chin. He wore a horizontally striped naval T-shirt and sported a naval beret at a jaunty angle. Sibénaler was an ex-naval officer and he ran a tight ship. When the French navy was disbanded with the German occupation he took to the forest. He seemed a solid character and it seemed natural that he was in charge.

We used first names only. I knew only a few of the last names until after the war. One young fellow would sit to the side and play a mouth organ, the soft, haunting melodies wafting around the clearing and lifting on the breeze. James Grunenwald was storybook handsome with wavy hair parted high. It was gingery brown giving him the air of an Irishman. His freckled face was perfectly proportioned and with eyes that sparkled as he played. "I'd like to have a whirl at that," I said. I made a stab at the "Irish Washerwoman" and a couple of others I'd heard in the survey camps north of Timmins. This may have helped my cause because every now and then I would hear James say to one of the others, "I think maybe he is Canadian."

I was kept under close guard for those first three days. Then on the third day a buzz of excitement went through the camp. We could hear a car pull up on the road in the distance. After a while a well dressed man walked into camp escorted by two fellows with little Sten machine guns. He was wearing a civilian suit and obviously carried a lot of clout. This was the promised interview to see if I passed the test. Really wasn't a German undercover agent or whatever they suspected me of. We sat a little apart from the others

with only the two armed escorts. He offered no name and
no one introduced us. Only that he was the boss. He began
right away with the questions. What was my hometown?
What was my squadron? Who were my crew? Where had I
flown and what was the target? Where had I crashed and
why? I answered him easily enough. It seemed obvious to
me that I had been checked out and that he already knew
most of the answers. He seemed to be someone important
in the resistance movement who had been in touch with
London. I felt confident about that. But I didn't tell him
anything about the Belgian underground, what they had
done for me, or about staying in their camp.

After about an hour he said, "Fine. We will take care of
you. It won't be long now. You will soon be going home."
He turned to Sibénaler and said, "He's a Canadian airman
all right." He and his escorts left the camp. The men moved
forward and we shook hands all round. No one mentioned
the mysterious stranger. I was now accepted as part of the
Maquis unit. Sibénaler issued me a French carbine and
Charles Lebrun was back in business. Real business this
time. I was number nineteen in a *Maquis* unit of *La Fronte
Francaise de L'Intérieur.* Charles De Gaulle's Army of Resistance in France. I was put on the payroll and we signed a
pay book each week.

Jimmy Grunenwald and I had made friends. We took
turns playing the mouth organ during those long hours of
waiting. And we talked a bit about families. He asked how
old I was. I asked the date. It was August 4th, 1944, two
days before my birthday. "You're lucky," said Jimmy.
"We'll celebrate with *blanc mange.*" They did manage to
produce some Calvados apple brandy and we celebrated
with that. I was now twenty-three years old.

The next night they told me a raid was planned. A raid for important supplies, food. The *Maquis* camp had now moved to *Le Bois d'Iré-le-Sec,* a little closer to Torgny and the Belgium border. In a nearby village an old German World War I army officer, a *chef d'agriculture*, and a unit of about six elderly German soldiers were in charge of a Polish work unit. This was about a hundred Polish field workers who were getting in the crops through forced labour. Sibénaler said, "The chef is going in to the nearby town for supplies and we will raid his place while he is away. But be careful. He has a dog that will probably be left guarding the house."

I joined three others to make up the midnight raiding party for the two hour walk to the village. Sibénaler said, "For this raid you'll take pistols and revolvers, no rifles." They gave me a revolver. Of course, I took it in my left hand since I'm left handed. This seemed so unusual to them that I was called *"main gauche,"* or Lefty, from then on. We walked to the little village. Before entering it we cut the telephone lines to the house. I thought, 'Now I'm involved in a serious resistance operation with people who know what they're doing.' We walked right up to the front door and tried it, but no luck, it was locked tight. I went around the back by myself. Real cloak and dagger stuff. As far as I was concerned the back was where we should be for a break and enter. I pushed up the window at the back of the house, put my hand over the sill ready to crawl in and there was a dog licking my hand. I patted the dog, crawled in, made my way to the front door and let the gang in. The other three came in and we quickly started looking for loot. Food that is.

I headed for the kitchen in the back of the house. The first thing I spotted was a big earthen jar full of honey. I grabbed that. The others took a great big smoked ham, bread, and some other supplies. We headed out the door and soon came the complaint, "How are we going to take this ham along, it's too heavy to carry." One of the men rustled up a wheelbarrow from the back yard and we put the ham and all our loot in that. We headed out of the village. There was no one in sight as far as we could tell. None, except the dog, following us. My first *Maquis* operation and we had a comedy watch dog who not only let us in, licked my hand in friendship, but now wanted to come with us and share in the ham. This vicious dog that Sibénaler had warned us about. Actually he gave up on us about a kilometre out of town.

The route into *Le Bois d'Iré-le-Sec* was the *Chemin Jaune,* the yellow trail. So called because it was bright yellow sand. We thought we'd better not take the wheelbarrow along since it would leave a tell-tale trail. We ditched the barrow and staggered back into camp with the ham and all our other supplies. A good night's work. The food was manna from heaven. We all enjoyed it but for one fellow it had unforeseen consequences. A couple of nights later we came back from a raid about two in the morning. Once again the ham was cut in large slabs, a thick line of fat hanging on each slice, butter for our starving bodies. This we put on slabs of white bread and stood around the camp smacking our lips in delight. Marcel Pierre said, "I'm going to have some of Charles Lebrun's honey." He scooped out the honey on a slice of the white bread, and took a bite. Then his scream split the silence of the forest. He danced around screaming, at first unable to tell us what was wrong. A wasp had crawled into the honey during the afternoon, he had gulped it with his first bite, and it stung his tongue. His tongue swelled so badly that we worried about his health but he eventually recovered.

Two days later a raid was planned for Jametz, another nearby village where Polish workers were also being used in the fields. These raids were one of the means the resistance had of getting food, and cigarettes. Cigarettes were a highly-prized commodity. The guards would be out in the field at the noon hour, guarding the workers, so the raid was planned for that time. Jemetz was a two hour walk. The plan was to rush in, get what we could, and rush out. Like Indians in a wild west show we sneaked into the village in single file, behind the shed, then rushed the target house, our guns at the ready. A lone Polish lady, the cook, stood in the kitchen, defenceless. My job was to guard her. I was carrying my carbine. I cocked the gun and said, "*Nicht spazieren.*" Don't move, don't walk around. She spoke German and I hoped she understood. I looked at her. 'Mom wears her long hair up in a bun at the back just like this lady. Mom wears an apron just like that. I hope she doesn't move. She looks like my mother. I can't kill her. I can't shoot. Dear God, don't let her move.' I needn't have worried. She was frightened and just stood there staring at me.

The rest of the raiding party ran upstairs and down checking for food, money and anything else we could use. About five or six minutes and it was over. We rushed out. One of the crew said "*Voila les Boches.*" And in the distance, down by the river, we could see the Germans waving their arms. They started running towards us. They were about a kilometre or more away. We raced to the woods, heading back to camp. We laughed like devils at our success for most of the way home. I was buoyant. This was like playing cowboys and Indians, for real. I felt good. We hadn't fired a gun. We hadn't been shot at. Yet.

We moved camp again, this time just a few kilometres west to le Bois de Juvigny. We didn't want packed trails leading into our camp. We wanted fresh forest. We almost never lit fires. I was living in French now and had no trouble communicating. My health was still poor. The scabies had managed to take over again since I had no hope of keeping clean. And my body was ravaged by boils. But I kept up to the group as much as I could. Sometimes I would stay back in camp, if just a few went out on a raid, but if everyone went then I was there too. This *Maquis* unit was doing some fighting. And the next raid was for just that purpose. It would be my first of the war. The Germans were retreating as the Allies advanced north through France from the Normandy landing. And this would be an ambush on some of the Germans in retreat.

CHAPTER TWELVE

THE HOT SUNNY DAYS OF THAT EARLY AUGUST didn't penetrate into the cells, in the depths of *La Citadelle Sainte Walburge* in the city of Liège, Belgium. For Albert Paul there was no sunshine. The small, iron-grilled window set high in the wall revealed the dingy cell to daylight, but there were no sunny rays. This was an emaciated Albert Paul. His nose more prominent than ever in a face, pale and haggard. His body showed the signs of beatings and torture after three months of Nazi prisons, first in Arlon and now at *La Citadelle,* the ancient fortress in Liège in central Belgium. He had held out with courage against it all. Now he and the other prisoners had heard the whispers. They knew that it wouldn't be long before the Allies would enter the city. But would there be enough time for Albert Paul?

That fateful day in May when he was captured by the Gestapo was the culmination of a long fight against the enemy. Albert had grown up in the little village of Torgny in the southern corner of Belgium, touching the southern tip of the Ardennes. In the province of Luxembourg. He joined the gendarmes in 1939 at the age of twenty-four. Just a year later in May 10, 1940 the German war machine rolled into Belgium. Albert was in the forefront of fighting with the gendarmes, and took a machine gun bullet in his jaw. He hovered between life and death, and spent eleven months in hospital recovering. When Albert returned to his home province he was assigned to the seven member Etalle brigade of the gendarme. He also, secretly, joined the resistance, the Independence Front in 1941. He was part of the *"Armée Secrète Ardenne," secteur sept, zone cinq*. The Secret Ardenne Army, sector seven, zone five. With his sturdy physique, his daredevil attitude, his patriotism and courage, he made a natural leader of the local unit. He was a wilful man, and paid little attention to his own safety. He was obsessed with the freedom of his country. Although he cared for his family and his men, his country's freedom was first and foremost.

It wasn't long before he and his men were deeply involved in sabotage, investigating collaborators, receiving and storing arms and other supplies from the Allies. He married Cécile Ravet. She also played a role in the resistance work. Their home in Etalle became a safe house for Allied soldiers and airmen. And Cécile knew of the dangers awaiting Albert when he and his men went out on raids at night. Albert and Cécile had set up an alliance with their neighbors, the Messiens. They were able to find food supplies for the "visiting guests" on farms in the area. A local butcher Manu Briquemont supplied much of the meat.

In the early days of May, 1944 Albert still had the Canadian airman James Moffat, the British airman Bill Jones, and Cécile's brother, René Ravet hidden in his house. Vital had warned his brother that the Gestapo were getting wise to him. Vital urged Albert to run for it. As usual Albert had his own plans. He was in the midst of a job that he thought needed to be done. In the early morning hours of May 17 he was on gendarme duty, on bike patrol in Buzenol, about four kilometres away from Etalle. The Gestapo had been keeping a watch on him and stepped in for the capture. A convoy of army trucks and Gestapo cars pulled up. The soldiers shoved him into one of the cars, heavily guarded, and drove to his house in Etalle. Eighty Germans encircled the village and the Paul house. The three men in the upstairs bedroom jumped out of the window just seconds ahead of the Gestapo. Cécile, clutching baby Monique, fled to the Messiens next door. The Gestapo shot the English aviator Bill Jones in the leg. Both Canadian aviator James Moffat and Cécile's brother René Ravet escaped. Moffat running for his life on his own, and Ravet to a small resistance group in the nearby woods.

The Gestapo continued their hunt for Cécile. The Messiens were terrified, both for her and for themselves. They helped her dress up as an old woman, with long dress and kerchief. The Germans finally gave up the hunt and headed out with their prisoners. By afternoon the plans were made. Baby Monique was left with the Messiens and Cécile fled Etalle on a bicycle. She went straight to Halzanzy. For eight days she hid there with the convent nuns. Arrangements were made with Vital. Marie-Claire Paul travelled to Etalle to bring back the baby. She and Vital, along with Cécile's parents, raised Monique for four months until the Allied liberation. The Gestapo was determined to capture Cécile as well. They soon turned the hunt to Halanzy. Once more Cécile mounted her bike and escaped to the *Hospice de Veillards*, about 100 kilometres away. The Germans soon found the baby and kept a close check to see if the mother was drawn back to the area by the baby's presence. The elderly grandparents were constantly afraid that the Germans would take Monique away and hide her. But this didn't happen. The *religieuses,* the nuns of charity, at the Hospice, hid Cécile for four months until the end of the war in Belgium that September.

The Germans took Albert Paul and Bill Jones to Arlon, about forty kilometres away. This capital city of Luxembourg province had been headquarters for the Germans in that area since the occupation. There they had their military prison. The two men were immediately separated. Their interrogation was long and rough. The Gestapo used the beatings, and torture that were their trademark.

In this portion of a letter to Vital Paul dated 5 May 1947 Bill Jones picks up the story for Albert and himself. "...I was taken to the front of the house where Albert was guarded by the Boche outside the car. We were then tied to each other and a Jerry started to ask me questions. I did not understand him and Albert told him I was an English airman. As soon as he heard that he just said: *"Englander-pisine"* English piss, and gave me a blow which knocked me to the ground. I was going to retaliate, but a sharp tug from Albert undoubtedly saved my life as the Jerry had swung his rifle up and I knew it was hopeless to try to even up... Albert and I were not allowed to speak to each other. We were then taken by car to Arlon where we were parted, the Germans taking Albert in one room and me in the other. That is the last I saw of Albert and I can only say that throughout the whole time he was very cool, quiet and calm as though it was an every day event. He was certainly a credit to Belgium and deserved of the highest honours, as I could gather from the scraps of conversation that I understood, that he was only concerned with my safety, thinking nothing of his own life. The Germans apparently thought I was a spy but Albert I think, convinced them that I was not and this I think played a large part in saving my life. However as I said that is the last time I saw Albert, and throughout the whole time they were questioning him and threatening him...

As for myself, I was in for a rough time and I knew it... they tried coaxing flattering and threatening me, with a stroke or two of a whip thrown in but I am glad to say that I could not and would not betray the faith of my many Belgian friends - giving them only my name rank and forces number which was supposed to be sufficient. The interpreter really got wild and wanted to know how long I had been in Etalle - if we had had any visitors - if I had been anywhere before I came there and hundreds more questions. I realized that if I answered any of these questions I should be endangering the lives of all the people whose hands I had passed through and so I answered that I was only in the place where I was captured and hadn't seen anyone or contacted anyone else. The rest of the questions I refused to answer and so I was put in a cell in Arlon jail. For a week I had nothing to eat from the Germans and I was dragged out from time to time for further questioning and on one occasion was taken outside to be shot. By that time I did not care what happened to me as I had had no food for several days and was very weak. However they brought me back in the cell again and must have given me up as hopeless at Arlon.

From that time onwards I was taken to four or five Gestapo places in Belgium with more or less the same treatment as at Arlon and I eventually finished up at Brussels. I being a human wreck and the Germans still no wiser for all their questionings threats and ill treatment. That was my only satisfaction, and I was proud to think that I had not let my friends in Belgium down.

At Brussels I was placed among other captured airmen and eventually arrived in a prisoner of war camp some two months after my capture. As I have said before I think I owe my life to Albert for what he said before we were parted... - signed, your old friend, Jacques Lenoir (W. Jones)."

Word spread quickly in Etalle village and the surrounding community that a hero of the *Maquis* had been captured. Details of the *Maquis* operations were not well-known, and certainly not bruited about by those who did know, but nearly everyone was well aware of Albert's activities. He was a member of *l'A.S.A., l'Armée Secrète* - Ardennes. In fact many people were also helping the cause. It was a blow to have such a dedicated patriot as Albert taken. The disappearance of the two men, Moffat and Ravet and the successful escape by Cécile Paul, were events to celebrate. But a pall fell over the entire area with the capture of Albert. The Etalle brigade of the gendarme was devastated. In fact for many of them their lives were on the line, depending on any possible disclosures to the Gestapo. The area had been hit by many German raids during the past four years of occupation, but none so devastating.

The Nazis knew that they had in their hands a major resistance leader and they were determined to get as much information from him as possible. In the spring of 1944 they already knew that the Allies were planning a major offensive. They knew that supplies were being dropped behind their lines. And they knew that the sabotage being carried out by the *Maquis* was costing them, in supplies and equipment, also in soldiers. They suspected that the gendarme was involved. They also believed that Albert Paul had information that they needed to wipe out resistance in Luxembourg province. They intended to get it.

They systematically beat and tortured Albert. Word got out that the beatings were occurring. Even on Sunday. This horrified the faithful and pastoral Roman Catholic community. The word was also spread that Albert had revealed nothing about his resistance group. No names. No places. No activities. He remained silent. The family and community closed ranks. And waited.

The spring days lengthened but the days remained dark at Arlon prison. For six weeks Albert endured the rough treatment. Then the date was set. He was slated to go before a military tribunal on June 27, 1944. The man in the prisoner's box was pale and thin, showing signs of his beatings. But his tall frame still held the dignity of the old Albert Paul. The proceedings were short. And the decision of the *"Conseil de Guerre,"* the military judges, was final. The ruling of the *Oberfeld Kommandantur - Haut Commandement Militaire* in the occupied region. The *"Tribunal de l'O.F.K. 589, Service Auxiliaire d'Arlon,"* ruled that Albert Paul had favoured the enemy, ie the Allies, was a *"franc-tireur,"* a sniper, had stored arms, and undertaken acts of sabotage.

He was sentenced to death. By firing squad.

Twenty days later, on July 17, he was moved. Shackled hand and foot, Albert Paul was taken north by convoy to Liège. The Gestapo had set up headquarters at 192 *Boulevard d'Avroy* in the city, and taken over the ancient *Citadelle* as their prison.

This 700 year old fortress, *Citadelle Sainte Walburge,* stood on one of the gentle, grassy hills encircling Liège, its ramparts overlooking the city. It had been first constructed in 1255 but had seen many changes over the centuries. Its octagonal battlements soon became a landmark, in a prominent position above the city of Liège. Each century brought changes. In the seventeenth it had been partially destroyed by the French, and rebuilt. The powder house became a chapel, its arched windows like half moons. Napoleon came and went. In the nineteenth a new entrance portal was built, with the same gentle arch. A boulevard encircled the ramparts of the fortress. Ivy clung to the sides. During the German occupation of Belgium in WWI La *Citadelle* had been taken over by the enemy, and once again in WWII.

The convoy passed through the shadowed, arched stone entrance into the open courtyard. The prisoner was taken through the outer square to the armoured door of Cell Block 24 which was also guarded by barbed wire fencing. Through the door to a narrow corridor leading to the cells. The tiny room, about six by twelve feet, held a cot, and a table with a tin basin. The prisoners sometimes used these tables to stand on, to see through the door window, into the corridor or through the barred window outside. At the top and bottom of one wall there were air holes, covered with perforated metal plates. Outside, the windows of the three story cell block were guarded with heavy, thick bars, leaving little space for light to enter. It was here that Albert Paul would await his death sentence.

In the Nazi occupied countries a *"Gestapo Abteilung"* had been established under the direction of a commandant of security police, the SS. But after 20 July, 1944, a special Commission of the Gestapo was set up to prosecute members of the resistance. In its own brutal way. A German called Strauch commanded the security police in Liège in 1944. He was assisted by Lucke, Knausseder, Krause, Villerhause, and the Belgian collaborators Brab, Hesterman, L'Honneux, Tierlynck, Verhofstaed, Huet, and Cristel. Records and survivor reports show that life at *La Citadelle Saint Walburge* was cruel, and torture unremitting, for those who had fought to liberate Belgium.

The Germans had installed a modern kitchen in the depths of the fortress. But for the prisoners the food could be a cup of blackish, stinking liquid, possibly cabbage or rutabaga soup. Sometimes sauerkraut. The door to the torture chamber was diagonally across the square from Block 24. Inside, a series of iron rings hung ominously on the wall. In each series, two for the wrists and two for the ankles. In the centre of this grim chamber was a table where the prisoner could be secured. A wooden block. Above this a tin can suspended by a wire. Drop by drop the water would fall on the victim's face. A form of the Chinese water torture. Outside this chamber an arched, armoured door opened onto a dark stone tunnel, running through to a grassed enclosure. Here, stark against the green of the grass and blue of sky, stood the *"poteaux d'execution,"* the execution stakes. About ten execution stakes.

Robert Gendarme was a m*aquisard* in 1941. Captured, condemned to death, imprisoned at *La Citadelle*. Gendarme had suffered beatings as well, some by rubber truncheon on the bottoms of his feet. He escaped *La Citadelle*, got out of Belgium and later fought as a volunteer against Germany. But while in Block 24 he watched from his cell as his friends were taken along the corridor to the torture chamber, returning with bloodied bodies and blackened eyes. Gendarme wrote of his experiences. He told of a Belgian soldier, a non-commissioned officer, Julien Maka. In the neighbouring cell to the left. Despite beatings Maka refused to confess to resistance work, but a comrade confessed, and Maka was condemned to death. Gendarme, and others in the cells, also watched as his friend Jamart went to his execution. A German soldier carried the black silk handkerchief. Jamart, handcuffed and held by two German *gendarmes*, was next. The prisoner had a white cloth square pinned on his jacket, just on the left of the chest. Over the heart. A lame priest, the prison chaplain *l'Abbé Voncken*, followed behind, carrying a crucifix. Jamart walked calmly. Gendarme wrote "…we are powerless to prevent his sacrifice. We have not a word to help in his walk; clinging to the bars, I weep with powerless rage. He disappears from our eyes; a moment of calm, then a round of gun fire enters the walls of the battlements; none of us says a word, our breath suspended, we await the result of the tragedy."

Vital Paul had some standing in the community. Some influence. He used it all and managed to get in to the German military prison in *La Citadelle* at Liège to see his brother. For Vital it was a sad sight. Instead of the handsome, happy-go-lucky Albert he saw a brother who had lived a lifetime in eight weeks. Had suffered the full force of Nazi terror. His body was badly damaged. But Vital could see that Albert still had the optimism, the courage and stamina, as well as a great deal of faith. Vital came away wholeheartedly worried about his brother. He tried to use his influence again. He asked to have Albert's sentence changed to life in prison with hard labour. The German High Command refused.

For Albert the visit was a reason to rejoice. He wrote a letter intended for Cécile, his family and friends. It was dated Liège, July 29. "*Ma cher Cécile, ma petit Monique*, dear mother, father, brothers and sisters and all the family and friends. I am happy to be able to give you my news, my health is good and my morale also and I hope that you are all the same. That Cécile stay courageous and begin life well again and that mama doesn't worry. The visit by Vital gives me great pleasure, I believe to see him again Friday but it is without doubt for the last time. That he continues to work with ardour, I have hope and confidence. Pray much for me.

Will you make me a little parcel and it will be with pleasure that I receive it. I have no need of soap you will… but send my razor. If you need anything will you speak to the gendarmes at Etalle. I suppose that my little Monique is very well-behaved and is growing a great deal. I have her photo on my table, it softens my condition (here). I would love to receive a photo of my little *Cécile mais surtout une avec le sourire*. But especially one with a smile. Everyone stay very courageous, especially Cécile and Mama. Say hello to Gabriel and all the family and friends and to the comrades of Etalle. …Christian and Annie… I finish by embracing you all with all my heart. *Albert. Au revoir*".

Vital did travel to Liège, to *La Citadelle*, once more to see his brother but he returned to Halanzy in despair. "I cannot go to see him any more," he told his wife Marie-Claire. "I cannot see him like this. I cannot look at his condition. I cannot go back."

But Albert Paul had not despaired. He had not lost faith in *"la lutte,"* the struggle. He wrote *"La lutte que j'ai menée était belle…* the struggle that I have made was good and it consoles me, for I see the enemy who runs away everywhere; *les echos de notre VICTOIRE,* the echoes of our VICTORY will make themselves heard beyond the walls of the prison. I am happy to know, before I leave, *que vous resterez belges,* that you will remain Belgium!"

13 August 1944, the night before his death, Albert Paul spent with the Roman Catholic priest, *l'Abbé Voncken*. This

cell had a stool and an altar. It was for those condemned to death.

Albert Paul did get to see the early morning sky over his "beloved" Belgium again. Just before six in the morning of 14 August the guards brought him, handcuffed, along the corridor past the cells of Block 24. *L'Abbé Voncken* followed with the crucifix. They walked through the dark tunnel to the grim, grassed area containing the *"poteaux d'execution."* The firing squad was already assembled, the black handkerchief was put on the prisoner. The shots rang out at 6:10 A.M. Albert Paul died for his country. Cécile and Monique lost a husband and father. The resistance lost a brave leader. But the province of Luxembourg gained a hero and martyr.

Three days later the German Conseil or tribunal, sent the death notice to the registry office through the mayor of Etalle.

"A Monsieur le Bourgmestre a Etalle (Arrondt Virton)Le Belge Paul, Albert, born the 7.6.1915 at Torgny, last lived at Etalle, employed by the *gendarmerie*, had been condemned to death by decision of 27.6.1944 *du Conseil de guerre de l'O.F.K. 589 -Service auxiliaire d'Arlon -,* for favoring the enemy, having been a sniper, for sabotage and storage of arms. The sentence was executed by firing squad, 14 August 1944, in *la citadelle de Liège.* The present communication is made to permit the amending of the civil state register. It is asked at the same time to notify the spouse of the above-named. This lady will be equally advised that she is able to take possession, upon receipt, of some objects having belonged to her husband, by speaking to the military war prison of the *citadelle of Liège.* -signature illegible. *Conseiller de tribunal de guerre."*

Twenty-four days after Albert's execution the Allies liberated the city of Liège. The Americans entered *La Citadelle* on 8 September 1944. The Germans had fled on 7 September. But three days before their retreat they executed seventeen more prisoners at *La Citadelle*. In Albert Paul's cell the Americans found two letters he had written to Cécile and his family. He had also left a note for *l'Abbé*. "To Monsieur the chaplain. Remembrance of the last night of the *"maréchal des logis'* of *gendarmerie* Albert Paul, born at Torgny 7 June 1915, shot at Liège the 14-th August 1944. My thanks and my best remembrance. *Paul Albert, gendarme at Etalle. Province de Luxumbourg, Belgique.* -signed *Paul.*"

CHAPTER THIRTEEN

THE MAQUIS RAIDS WERE AIMED at harassing the soldiers who were retreating north east toward Germany, in front of the Allies advancing from the Normandy landing. We could often hear the artillery in the distance. We had no intelligence about the retreat, we just took the chance that some Germans would be coming along our main roadway. That day we made our way to the main highway nearby, armed with our rifles and lugging along the one and only machine gun. The machine gun was set up on the roadside embankment, but hidden in the woods. Two men stayed with it, Sibénaler was the gunner and he had a helper. The idea was that they would cover our escape if we ran into trouble. Sibéneler had the rest of us stretched out on either side of the highway. That was the part I didn't like. Particularly since I was with the group on the wrong side of the highway, away from our forest retreat. I thought this was dangerous since if there was trouble we'd have to cross the highway to get back to the forest. It put us at additional risk. But when we arrived at the spot we lay down in the ditches. Just lay down in the ditches beside the roadway. We waited. And waited. An hour passed. Then a convoy of German trucks and cars passed. Then we waited again. A car came along carrying three men in German uniforms. Sibénaler yelled, *"Tirez."* We all stood up and started firing.

The car crashed into the ditch. Everybody in the car was badly wounded. Or dead. Or dead two minutes later. The adrenaline was running. I was so excited, so caught up in the action. My heart was pounding fifty times its normal speed. It was the most amazing thing. This was no "fly high in the sky and peer down at a target through cloud cover" kind of action. My heart was pumping and my mind was in a whirl. Waiting in the ditch, then jumping up and firing at a human being for the first time. Nowhere near the same as firing machine guns at night at an almost invisible target. These people were in front of you and you had to try to hit them. I was surprised at the rush of adrenaline, and the sort of excitement that took hold of me. I was able to perform as I had done when we were shot up over Texel. But the nearness of being right on the ground. I was surprised at the excitement of that. I guess we are hunters after all. We all rushed over, grabbing money, guns, ammunition. Then we ran. We headed back to camp. The frightening elation of the adventure, or experience, rolled on for hours, at least four or five hours.

We had no way of keeping prisoners. I understood that was the rationale, if there was one. The men had shot any survivors. I don't think I could have done it. I never knowingly shot anyone. I shot at the vehicle from a fair distance by the roadside. Others ran up and shot the survivors. I don't know what I would have done, who I would have shot, if my life depended on it. But I certainly would have.

After we returned to camp a fellow called "Barbeau" showed up. He wore a beard and a pistol in a holster strapped around his waist. He said, "Look at my pistol" and gave it a slap, shooting himself in the leg. Barbeau fell down screaming and threw the gun and holster away. I picked it up and asked if I could keep it. "Hell, yes," he said and that's how I got my German pistol. It was a copy of the .45 pistol that American officers carried.

We moved camp right away after the highway operation. It wasn't much of an effort because we had no real "camp." We just put on all our clothes, carried any food we might have, and found a new spot in the forest. This time we moved maybe fifteen kilometres away. The Germans would certainly put out a search party and we wanted to be out of sight. It was night by the time we came to the new spot. Tall maple, oak and beech trees towered overhead. The forest bed was damp underfoot. And something was crunching as I walked. "What's that?" I asked. "Oh, escargots," came the answer. The next day I could see. Great big snails, about half the size of my fist, hanging on the side of the trees. At night they would go to ground, foraging for food. I had been stepping on them. And we were sleeping among them.

One day in broad daylight we staged what came to be known to all of us as the "cigarette holdup." We went out about noon to an open field with a small highway running through it. Lucien Sibanéler again told us to hide along the side of the roadway. This time it would be risky since we were some distance from the forest on either side. There were valleys with farms at either end of the roadway, but we were isolated in the middle. We lay in the grass and the bushes for an hour or so. There was no traffic. Then a closed van approached. Sibenéler warned us again not to fire until he gave the order. As the van approached Lucien ordered us to jump in front and stop it. The two men inside were ordered out. They were upset, but soon laughing and shaking hands. The driver was the brother of one of the *Maquis*. Lucien had known the truck was coming but was not sure who would be driving. The two brothers caught up on the latest about the Germans, and how their family was coping. Two of us kept watch on the highway, and others unloaded some cartons of cigarettes, a good haul for us. Lucien told the driver to make a report to the authorities right away, that they'd been robbed by *"terroristes."* We waved our goodbyes and ran to the forest to put some distance behind us.

One night shortly after that James Grunenwald had gone into the city of Longuyon to see what information he could pick up that would help us plan another attack. We were awakened about three in the morning with the sound of machine gun and rifle fire. Everyone jumped up, fully dressed with guns at the ready. We could hear someone running down the pathway to the camp. It was Grunenwald. He had accidentally biked right through a German camp in the forest. He ditched his bike and ran through the woods to our camp. "The Germans have surrounded us," he said. They're all around. They're all over. They shot at me. There are trucks and armoured vehicles in the little glade at the edge of the forest."

Sibénaler immediately sent two men out one way to reconnoitre, and sent me and another fellow the other way. "Go the other way to the road, follow it around, check out *les Boches*, and hurry back." We headed out through the forest. I heard a vehicle coming along a road near the edge of the forest and we dashed behind a couple of trees. It was a jeep. A German officer stood in the front hanging onto the windshield. Two soldiers sat in the back. We kept to our hiding place. Before long the jeep drove back again. By this time it was almost daylight. We made our way to the edge of the glade. There was a surprise. About thirty trucks and jeeps were backed up under the trees around a clearing, with soldiers getting ready for breakfast. I thought, 'They're not looking for us. They're hiding under the trees for the day. The American bombers have been giving them hell. We have been hearing the artillery fire in the distance for the past few days so the American army can't be far behind. They'll take off tonight.' We went back and reported that the Germans didn't seem to be worried about looking for the Maquis but in saving their own skin. The others reported the same.

After some consideration and discussion Sibénaler made his decision. Close to dawn he said, "What we're going to do is, we're going to run out into the wheat field. Each person goes by himself. Just lie down in the wheat field. We'll stay there all day and wait for the Germans to leave." So we abandoned camp and spread out into the nearby wheat field. We left nothing behind. There was nothing there anyway just the piece of ground we slept on. I found myself a spot and lay down. Towards noon I could hear the clinking of tracks, like a carrier of some kind. I looked. There at the other end of the field I could see a Bren gun carrier, with three soldiers in it, break out from the forest. It headed across the wheat field and down to the village. 'Well,' I thought, 'he didn't hit anyone, I hope he takes the same route back.' And he did. We lay in the field all day. That night we could hear the convoy heading out. We went back to our forest retreat.

We'd had a bit of rain while at this camp, and it was drizzling again as we headed back. I said, "Why don't we stay in the little pine grove at the edge of the forest. We will have to be a little quieter, but we will stay drier, if not completely dry, under the tall pines. "Aha," they laughed, "the Indian from Canada." But they agreed. Even so we had to keep up our morning ceremony of burning off the wood ticks every day while we were in this particular forest. First thing, each of us would light a cigarette, get it going good. Then we'd drop our pants and apply the lighted cigarettes to the wood ticks which had their heads buried in the skin of our groins. It worked. But we had to do it every day. It made smoking a good thing.

It was about this time that our new leader arrived. He was Emile Randolet. Our new chief. It was now August 20, 1944 more than two months after D-Day. The Allies were advancing across Europe. On June 18 General Charles de Gaulle, who was directing the French resistance from his London headquarters, had given the order through the underground network. "All officers and non-commissioned officers are now back in the service." This gave the military officers in France two options. Wait for the Germans who would now round them up, or head for the bush and join the *Maquis*. After the occupation of France in 1940 many officers had gone home and taken up their old life as best they could. Lieutenant Emile Randolet had been chief of a section in the 132 Regiment of Fortress. His orders came in May of 1940, and he commanded two *Maginot* Line forts. He later lost his regiment, and regrouped at Saint Die, Vosges. But here the French surrendered their arms. The soldiers were taken prisoners of war. Randolet refused to do this. He headed off with some soldiers from the Polish army. He returned to his sister's home at Jarny. He was a professor of mathematics in the college at Longuyon. The college retreated to Pierrepont fearing the Allied bombing of the rail yards at Longuyon. It was here that he heard de Gaulle's call for officers to go back to active duty. He had already been working in the resistance with Grunenwald, making false papers. And Grunenwald had gone to see him, asking him to take command of our unit.

Randolet was a heavy set man. Tall, straight, with a strong face. His hair had receded giving him a high forehead. Dark eyes were set wide over a nose and mouth that were almost Slavic in width and thickness. He came into camp with a sergeant at his heels. This was Lucien Hennequin who had been leading a resistance group which had been attacked by the Germans. Six of them had been killed. Now Hennequin joined us. He was a slight, quiet fellow. Both of them brought the air of the army about them. Now we had an airman, myself, a naval officer Sibénaler, and two army personnel. This meant taking more chances, attacking the enemy now that news of the Allies' advance was in the air. Now we would go searching for trouble.

Most of the group members were young men who had run away from German work camps, or who had been dodging the Germans by living in the woods. Robert Kesseler and Gino Norris were examples of the young people who had had their schooling interrupted by war. At fifteen they were left without school or work since the ironworks were also closed. Then Kesseler was hired by the city of Longwy in north western France, gathering wood, picking up garbage, finding the dead in the valley of Coulmy under

Romain. One beautiful day Kesseler and Norris decided to hoist the French tricolour that they had found in the Gouraincourt school. Others joined them, and with the bravado of the very young they decided to raise their flag on the German commandant's flagpole in the Longwy-Bas square. The young people were arrested. In spite of efforts by the mayor of Longwy, the seven young boys were sentenced to six months in prison at Nancy. Once released Kesseler and Norris became friends with Hennequin and Gilbert Lambiney both of whom were police agents. All four decided to join the *Maquis*. They travelled to Longuyon by train, hidden under parcels in the mail car. They joined our resistance group while it was still headed by Sibénaler.

Marcel Jonette had been unable to rejoin his unit in North Africa. He had returned to Tellancourt where he and his friends Joseph Pawlak and René Warion were carrying out some clandestine operations at night. During the day they had been working on a farm. They were accused of stealing wheat from the farm, and were sent to prison at Nancy for two months. Jonette then joined the *Maquis*.

One day I heard Randolet and the group discussing a German radar station they'd heard about. Radar was new. No one realized what it was. As the only airman, I explained how radar worked and the danger it posed for our bomber command and fighter pilots. "It would be a good idea to knock it out," I said. Of course the radar station itself included barracks of soldiers, bunkers and other buildings. We certainly didn't have the strength to attack it. I suggested we cut the telephone lines and any power lines we could find. Randolet set us to cutting the power lines then we headed back to camp. This we did by daylight.

A couple of days later three of us went back to check if

the lines were still cut. They had been repaired. When we reported this to Randolet he said, "Oh, we'll fix their clock." He sent a couple of the men to cut the lines again, at a place we hoped would be difficult to find. This time we left three guys to wait and watch. They reported. "Two soldiers came along on bicycles and said, 'Here's where the lines are cut.' We shot them. One yelled for mercy, that he had children at home. We killed them both." The cruelty of it hit me with a shock. We had not been moving camp much with Randolet in charge, but we moved that time thinking it would get too hot for us there.

I had grown to like Grunenwald. He seemed to be a cleaner, gentler soul than many of the others. He and I talked, as much as I could get along in French at the time. And of course we shared the mouth organ. Grunenwald now had another bicycle. This gave him the job of checking up on the Germans in our territory. The Germans had a unit stationed in Longuyon which was his hometown. Every few days Grunenwald would cycle into Longuyon to see what he could learn.

One day he went into town searching for more arms for the *Maquis* group. He stopped at his mother's home. The woman living next door saw him and ran screaming into the street, "*Un terroriste, un terroriste.*" The Germans gave chase. Grunenwald pedalled away as fast as he could, but not fast enough. He was shot down. When Grunenwald didn't return we soon learned the story of what had happened. Randolet said, "I want a volunteer to take care of that collaborator." I thought, 'This is war after all. The fellow I have made friends with in this group has already been killed.' I reached into my pocket and put my hand on the mouth organ which I often borrowed from Jimmy. Jean

Martin volunteered. He came back a little later and told his story. Martin had gone directly to Madame Grunenwald's neighbor. He said, "Madame, you know what you have done." Put his gun to her head and shot her. It was August 24, 1944 the day James Grunenwald died.

Denis Trussard had been a friend of James Grunenwald. He joined the *Maquis* just after Jimmy's death. He and Marcel Pierre looked up Jean Martin before arriving at Iré-le-Sec. René Warion and Joseph Pawlack followed, completing our group.

Randolet now set up some lines of communication. Our runner was a boy of about ten or twelve years of age. Every couple of days he would come to camp. He had messages for Randolet telling us something of what was going on with German movements. And, of course, we could hear the Allies' guns in the distance.

We continued our harassment of enemy traffic on the main highway. But here Randolet's strategy made a little more sense to me. We all stayed on the same side of the highway so that we had easy access to our escape route. One day Randolet deployed the machine gun at a corner in the road, where there was a forest just at the turn. It was up high enough that it could spray the roadway to protect us. Sibénaler and his partner at the machine gun also had rifles. The rest of us were deployed at the ditch area with our Sten guns and pistols. I was still carrying my little French carbine. Randolet hadn't brought any extra rifle power with him, just his own pistol, and the sergeant carried a German *Mauser.* We used the same strategy as previously. We watched the convoys go by. Then waited. A German army truck came around the corner. Loaded with soldiers. We all opened up firing. Firing until the truck hit the ditch. It caught fire and burned. This meant we didn't get much loot. No ammunition. We depended on raids for our ammunition. No one survived and we did manage to get some guns.

Nearly every day now we would set up on a roadway and watch for a convoy. We had information from the courier boy, or we took our chances on finding some Germans. We hiked through the woods to whatever point seemed best. There was no time to think. The excitement of the moment kept my adrenaline pumping. After the raid we would make our way however many kilometres back to camp as fast as we could. We ate and flopped onto the ground to sleep. Exhausted. I was far from well, with the constant plague of boils, and the scabies mites. Although I didn't realize it, I was suffering from malnutrition as well.

One morning about eight o'clock the boy ran into camp from the village. He handed Randolet the message then quickly left. Randolet turned to us. "Ah, there are ten or fifteen Germans hiding in a town called Quincy. We're going to capture them." I looked around. There were eighteen of us. It was broad daylight. A raid on the Germans in broad daylight. 'This is asking for trouble,' I thought but made ready to go with everyone else. We all put on our arm bands with the letters F.F.I. showing that we were part of De Gaulle's army. It was really no protection if the Germans caught us because we knew we'd be shot anyway but it added to the bravado, created an *esprit de corps*. We knew that the Germans didn't want to surrender to the French resistance groups. They were waiting for the Americans to advance and would surrender to them. But Randolet had a different idea. He wanted to capture some Germans. He was a regular army officer who had suffered defeat. Had had to sit out the war for four long years. Watched his country submit. Knew of the atrocities happening all around him while he quietly taught school. Now was his chance. He, Randolet, would take the enemy and personally deliver them to the Americans. We headed out walking. There was a different feeling about this raid. We were actually going to capture some of the enemy. A certain determination. A certain *"joie de guerre."* But also apprehension. Gino Norris and Roger Broggi were of Italian background. Their families had originally come to France and Belgium to work in the iron mines. Now, as young men, they were hiding to escape the German work camps. Roger Broggi was a chubby faced fellow, with an easy smile. His thick dark hair was combed straight back from a round face. Roger's home was now in Mangiennes, France. He stuck close to me as we hiked along. Like glue. He worried about a raid on the Germans in broad daylight. He worried about trying to capture trained soldiers. Trained German soldiers. Well, I had all the same worries. But at least I had had some military training.

So Roger stayed at my side, to follow my lead. About noon we arrived at Quincy. The village nestled in a valley, its houses and buildings scattered along the side of a river which curved through the valley and out the other end. As we approached we came up beside part of the *Maginot* Line. One of the big cement bunkers that the French had built as a defence against the Germans after World War I. It was about ten feet high and forty feet wide. We were on the main road to Quincy. Randolet stopped us just in front of the bunker. Apple trees lined both sides of the roadway. We were looking down the hill into the village. Randolet put Hennequin in charge of half of the group. Hennequin took eight men and went down to the river to cross over, and cut off any of the fifteen Germans who might try to escape. We watched them go to the left, then cross over the river, and start toward Quincy the back way.

We continued on the main road to the village. We were about 300 feet from the first house, when we saw a man coming up the hill pushing his bicycle. He stopped beside us. We must have looked a rag tag group. A little Free French army, tattered and unwashed. Carrying sidearms, rifles and our one machine gun. This fellow told Randolet that he was in the intelligence section of the resistance. "Oh, it's good to see you guys operating in the daylight. Like a real army." Randolet answered. "Yes. We're going to capture the Germans. Where are they?" "Oh," he said, "*Ce n'est pas difficile.* It's not difficult. Over there on the hill there's about twenty. They have a machine gun and mortar. And down in the bushes there, about 200 yards down, there's a machine gun. Over there, on the hill over there, another machine gun and mortar. And over here another machine gun and mortar. And down in the city hall, that big building there, there's about 200 more Germans."

We looked in horror at our comrades below, walking in innocence along the low land toward the back of the village. Randolet was frantic. He began to yell and wave his arms. "Let's get out of here. Get out of here. Let's get away. *Echappez.*" The Germans opened up with everything they had. I'm sure they thought we were the forward party of a large army. The first blast our little group got was from the bushes just below us, so described by our friendly informer. Fortunately the machine gun was zeroed in on the bunker behind us. They obviously thought if there was to be an attack the soldiers would hide behind the cement bunker. Of course there we were about ten feet below it, on the road. In front of the bunker. Foolish luck again. Our naiveté. I hit the dirt. So did Roger beside me. I looked up and there was Randolet running. He wore a big black hat for protection against the sun. A bullet hit his hat and it went flying. He slid behind the bunker. The German machine gun was aimed a little high. Apples, like raindrops, fell bouncing on the highway as bullets hit the trees on both sides of the road.

CHAPTER FOURTEEN

I MELDED TO THE GROUND, my face in the dirt, Roger at my side. Still. I lifted my head to look. Everyone had disappeared. The sounds of shooting filled the air. Machine guns firing from all directions. The mortar blasting away. I had never been under mortar fire in my life. Never even heard it. I was surprised that it wasn't loud. Just a continual POP, POP. But huge shock waves hit my ears. Fortunately the Germans were all still aiming at the bunker. Roger was the first to speak. "What are we going to do," he whispered, turning to me. "We're going to crawl along there. Get away from where they know we are. Then we'll start shooting from there." We managed to move along about 20 feet and get behind some bushes. Roger and I started returning fire.

Just then the Sibénaler's machine gun helper came running out from behind the bunker. The blood was running from his nose and ears. Our machine gun site had taken an almost direct hit from one of the mortars. He yelled at us, "We're the only ones here. They're all gone. Look." We looked. Our men were running through the field behind the bunker. The cows continued to graze peacefully, eating the potato tops. Ignoring the German fire and the escaping *Maquis*.

I yelled at Roger, "Let's get out of here." We crawled back across the roadway. It must have been about one o'clock. The Germans had been shooting for about 20 minutes. The sun was high and the heat of the day, fear, and tension of the battle had taken their toll. I was thirsty. I was so dry. There in the roadway was a puddle of rainwater. Yellow rainwater in the middle of the road. I crawled over to it and put my face down to get a drink. It tasted crystal clear. Then the three of us, Roger, the machine gunner's helper and I, started running. We avoided the field. By this time it was under fire. We followed the road back as much as we could before heading into the forest. We were the first three back at camp. I had lost Grunenwald's mouth organ and the two hand grenades from my pockets. But otherwise I was intact. The others began returning in twos and threes. Some not until midnight. And some not all. Each of those who did come back had a story to tell.

Denis Trussart was just eighteen years old. He was a fine-boned young man, with short, light brown hair. His home was in nearby Longuyon, and he had joined our unit just a few days after the death of his friend James Grunenwald. He was shaken by the day's events. "I had never before had to crawl for my life as I did today," he said. He and *un copain*, a buddy, were in the advance group that Randolet had sent across the river toward the back of the village of Quincy. When the onslaught of enemy action caught them in the crossfire, they hit the dirt and crawled to the flour mill near the river. They rushed into the mill and crawled into a huge flour bin. Trussart found himself trembling under the flour. "'We were afraid of being burned if the Germans decided to burn down the mill. I had a last grenade. I was saving it to blow us up, rather than burn." A man and his wife owned the mill. They were there when the Germans broke down the door, rushed in with their bayonets at the ready. The soldiers stuck bayonets into every bin and flour sack in sight. Fortunately they missed the Maquisards. Trussarts and his *"copain,"* made their way back to camp safely.

Marcel Pierre had also been down in the valley heading for the village when all hell broke loose. He made a quick decision. At the first firing, he jumped into the river. He stayed there, immobile and hidden in the reeds, for hours. He finally made his way back to camp about midnight. Randolet didn't show. He had been wounded high in the leg. He had taken a bullet. A couple of comrades had taken him immediately to a safe house. We didn't know at first how badly he was hurt, or if he'd be back. He was taken to Vigneulles, south of Montmédy. He was hidden in the house of an army adjutant called Jacquemin. A civilian doctor treated his bullet wound. He was lucky in that the bullet had missed an artery by a fraction of an inch.

It was September 2, 1944. A day that the disaster at Quincy claimed three of our *Maquis*. Three who had led the group entering the village the back way. Sergeant Lucien Hennequin of Pillon, France, who had served with the French army in Algiers, was shot and killed in the first round of gunfire at Quincy. René Warion was about eighteen or twenty years old. His short, trim hair cut, and square, clean shaven face, gave him the look of a kid just out of high school. And there was Joseph Pawlack of Tellancourt, France. Unfortunately for Pawlack and Warion they were only wounded at the Quincy entrapment. Joseph Pawlack had joined the group only two days before. He seemed older than most of us, except maybe Randolet. He was a fairly big man with a square jawed countenance, and an easy smile. His ears protruded slightly from the sides of his head. His slick, dark hair was parted almost in the middle, giving him a very European look. Pawlack and Warion were captured alive by the Germans. They were taken into Quincy. There the Germans had assembled about twenty of the most prominent villagers including the mayor and police chief, holding them hostage in the town hall. The Germans were afraid that we were an advance unit for a larger resistance group. They were holding the towns people as hostages. They had decided to shoot the villagers if we came back. When the fighting came to such an abrupt end they hung on to their wounded prisoners.

Next morning the Germans prepared to resume their retreat as the Allied guns resounded once more. And they had no room for prisoners. They assembled the villagers in the square. A ladder became the scaffolding in front of the town hall. And the wounded Pawlack and young Warion were hung before the horrified eyes of the people of Quincy. The 250 Germans resumed their retreat eastward to Germany. They hadn't lost a man.

The former naval lieutenant Sibénaler was back in charge. We could hear the guns, the Allies' guns, all the time now. The idea was to lie low and wait for the Americans. We hadn't long to wait for news. We just weren't sure if it was good news or bad news. Three days after the Quincy raid a runner came up from the village near Jametz. The boy was excited but unsure. "They've arrived. The soldiers are in the village." But, when questioned, he couldn't tell us if they were German soldiers or Americans.

Sibénaler took a cautious route. He decided we should reconnoitre carefully in case it was the Germans again. He picked a couple of guys to go take a look. Then he said to me, "You go with them. You'll know if they're Americans or not." The three of us walked about twenty minutes through the forest to the village, sneaking in the back way. We crept along beside the little buildings leading to the square. I put my head around to see what I could see. There he was. A sergeant sitting in the front seat of a jeep, with his feet up on the windshield! 'That's an American,' I thought. The Germans would never do that.' We ran into the square. Excited. I shouted, "What took you so long." He jumped up and stared. There was laughter all around as I told him who I was, and introduced my two companions. He was Sergeant William Ellis from North Carolina. He was with an American Recce, reconnaissance, outfit. The two *Maquis* headed back to the forest with the good news. I would liked to have gone back with them to say my goodbyes, and pick up some belongings such as a bayonet I had collected. But the sergeant said they'd probably be moving on and I'd better check with his lieutenant.

The jeep was parked in front of a house in the village square. So I made my way up the stairs to a small, low-ceilinged room. I walked in and there was the lieutenant sitting alone at the only table, eating a big, thick steak. I told him I was Flying Officer James Moffat of the R.C.A.F. "Would you like to sit down and have some steak?" he said. "No. No," I said. "We just had goose for our dinner in the forest." We had been given a goose and had cooked it on a camp fire. We were just finishing it at noon when the runner came. I had lived now for six months in French and was finding it difficult to think and speak in English. "How in God's name did you live?" he asked. "Oh. *Faire le guerre.*" The lieutenant stared.

I must have been a sight. I was wearing a German tunic that I'd picked up in a raid. I was carrying hand grenades in my pockets. A wide thick belt encircled my waist, and stuck in this was a German pistol. By now I was wearing hobnailed boots that I had picked up somewhere along the line. And I was carrying my French carbine. A scraggily beard covered my thin, pale face. "Well," said the lieutenant. "We can't have you travelling like that." He supplied me with a razor and uniform. And although I couldn't bathe it was heaven to strip off those rags and get into a clean outfit. Puttees, boots, steel helmet, the whole thing. In the pocket of the American uniform I found lieutenant bars. I put them on the epaulette and took the rank. And I joined the outfit. Leaving my *Maquis* friends behind.

This was an advance Recce outfit looking for bridges that had not been blown up by the Germans during the retreat. The idea was to ensure that the bridges weren't mined, or if they were, to secure them. Within fifteen minutes we climbed into the jeep to head north east. I got in the back with the rolls of toilet paper and chocolate bars. Liberation American style. The lieutenant rode up front with the driver. Both of them armed with Tommy guns and automatic pistols. Sergeant Ellis and I in the back with 50 calibre machine guns. I had also been issued a 25 calibre automatic 15 shot rifle. We headed the convoy of six jeeps and an M-8, an armoured vehicle with eight rubber wheels and a 37 millemetre cannon on it. We roared down the highway. I had no time to think about my turn of good luck.

We were passing through tiny villages as we headed toward the Belgian border. The convoy would slow down and we held our hands out. The villagers ran along side laughing, shouting and slapping our hands. Sometimes they threw apples at us, in sheer jubilation. Everyone celebrating the liberation. Sometimes the lieutenant shouted for champagne in his loud, jovial voice. In one village he got his answer. It wasn't exactly champagne. In fact it was nothing like champagne. It was prune whiskey. He passed the bottle around to the driver, Sergeant Ellis and me. Glug. Glug. Red hot molten lava ran down my throat. My innards burned with fire for the next half hour.

After about an hour we could see a fairly large town in the distance. And a bridge just before that town. A bridge still standing. The lieutenant called a halt in front of a roadside inn. "We'll stop here to see what we can find out." He turned to me. "You speak French. Go in there and talk to them. See what you can find out." I walked into the inn. The innkeeper was friendly enough and willing to tell us all he knew. "Are there any Germans around?" "*Mais oui*," he said. "Be careful. There are Germans at the bridge. And they have a gun set up there. Be careful." He shook his head. "On the far side of the bridge, the bridge is mined. The Germans will blow it up." I came out and reported this all to the lieutenant in good military style. "Ah," he said. "These Frenchies are all full of shit. Let's go." 'My God,' I thought, 'from the way the innkeeper talked he was telling the truth.' The convoy roared at sixty miles an hour toward the bridge. Our jeep in the lead.

CHAPTER FIFTEEN

IT WAS CHILLY IN THE BACK OF THE JEEP. The wind was blowing and we were travelling at about 100 kilometres an hour. And I knew there was a gun position up ahead. A German gun position. After Quincy I was jumpy. The innkeeper seemed an honest fellow. I felt he was telling the truth. Suddenly it was like someone tearing tar paper. Right by my ears. Scrooozzk. Screeek. My father had told me that you didn't really hear shells that were lobbed overhead, until they hit. But a flat trajectory shell sounded like tearing paper. And that's what I heard. Three, four, five times. It was the shells from the German gun going right past our ears. They kept firing, about twenty rounds. Nothing hit us. The American convoy was in a straight line and for some reason the gun couldn't hit the lead target. Us. The lieutenant yelled, "Stop. Turn around. We'll go around." The driver of the jeep turned into the ditch, backed up and headed back. The rest of the convoy followed. The M-8 was now aiming its 37 millimetre gun at the German position at the bridge. We never did see the Germans but their position was obvious from the firing. We raced back to the inn. The rest of the unit remained there to contact headquarters. We took a side road that led down to the river. I was hanging on and mentally saluting the innkeeper.

We weren't far down the side road before we hit another spot of trouble. The driver had just dipped down into a little gully when I saw a number of huge trees across the roadway. 'An ambush,' was my first thought. The driver stopped. I jumped out and in two seconds was behind a tree with a gun at the ready. The lieutenant went to have a look. He figured the Germans had been there but had given up this position for the one at the bridge. We had to turn again.

The lieutenant got his convoy in line once more. We pulled up at the small city of Montmédy. A French city fairly close to the Belgian border. The bridge had been blasted into the river. The River Chiers. We had stopped right beside a large home. It looked like a small hotel actually. The lady of the house came out to greet us. I was still acting as French interpreter. "Tell your officer to bring shovels. I will show him where the champagne is hidden," she said. I quickly translated this for the lieutenant. "Ah, that's what I've been looking for." A smile lit up his disgruntled countenance. He ordered the soldiers forward with their little, fold-over trench shovels. And we all went digging in her front yard. We dug up about twenty-five bottles of French champagne.

This was about three o'clock in the afternoon. I'd never drunk champagne before. I'd never walked four feet off the ground before. By five o'clock that's what I was doing. The lady of the house came to the interpreter again. "Tell the lieutenant. There's a special, big church service because of what happened yesterday. It's a service of thanksgiving. Maybe the officer would like to go." Then she told me the story of what had happened in Montmédy the day before.

The students at the university in Montmédy could hear the Allies' guns getting closer. They were excited by the coming liberation and decided to do a little liberating of their own. They had spread tacks and nails on the roadways. Tires were blown out as the German army began its retreat. The army commander ordered the students, as many as could be found, rounded up. The young people were lined up against a wall at the university. A firing squad was put in place, and the order was to shoot them all. But a German army doctor came to the rescue. He said to the commander, "The war is just about over. These are young people. They weren't in the resistance." He talked the commander out of it, and the Germans fled ahead of the American advance.

That had been the day before. This day, the day we arrived, the city had already planned its celebration of thanksgiving. Our host's son had been one of those university students. She was excited and pleased at the idea of having the liberators attend as her guests. "Oh yeah. We'll attend," said the lieutenant. So the lieutenant, Sergeant Ellis and I followed her to the church. The large church was packed. It was a Roman Catholic church, of course. The French priest walked up and down giving the eulogy of thanks. Thanks that the university students had been saved. Thanks that the Americans had come to liberate them. It was all in French. And, of course, the lieutenant couldn't understand a word of it. Had no idea what the priest was saying. It could have been Latin for all he knew. But he was in a champagne-induced, benign mood toward the French now. Every now and then he would sigh and whisper, "Isn't that marvellous. Isn't that marvellous."

That night we bedded down in an apple orchard, beside the River Chiers. We had to throw away the fallen apples to make a spot for our blankets. I couldn't really believe all that was happening. My good luck, bad luck of the past months seemed to be on the upswing. I knew I was still at risk, and could still get shot, but at least I was with an army unit, almost like being back on squadron. Someone would advise my family of my fate. And I could speak English, no doubt about what was being said. My only thought was to push on to Brussels and back to England. Now it seemed as if I might make it. I fell into an exhausted sleep.

We headed back to the Recce headquarters out in the forest. The reconnaissance unit had about 250 men. Convoys with jeeps and M-8's would go out in all directions hunting for trouble ahead of the regular troops. The good news was that the Americans had a field kitchen set up and we had a real hot supper. Beef hash, mashed potatoes, white bread and hot coffee. My first hot meal since staying with Madame Autphene in Couvreux months before.

I took the opportunity to talk to Bill Ellis about the actions of his leader, the lieutenant, attacking the bridge in such an aggressive manner, against all advice. "Oh, this is our fifth lieutenant since D-Day. The others were all killed. They don't know anything from beans," he said. "We try to save them, but we have a hard time." The sergeant laughed off this dilemma citing the Recce unit's dangerous job. "Our job is to go, go, go until the Germans fire on us. That's how we find them. So we have a high casualty rate," he said. He handed me an army blanket and I found a spot under the trees. *"Plus ca change, plus c'est la meme chose.'*

We were up early next morning ready to head out again. But then an aircraft landed in the next field. It was a British Auster. An R.A.F pilot stepped out and walked over to the colonel in charge of the American unit. Right away I had a plan. Here was a way back to England. 'Quick and easy,' I thought. I'd had enough of overland travel the past months, weeks, and days and I was an airman both at heart as well as in service. The colonel had other ideas. "No. You're staying with us. We'll take you back." The R.A.F. pilot stayed around for just a short time to complete his communication duty, then flew off.

We were now in a convoy of thirty jeeps, five M-8's and about 100 men from the Recce unit. We crossed the River Meuse at a ford above Sedan, since the bridge was out. The military traffic was non-stop. We followed a line of Sherman tanks with American infantry sitting atop them. These fellows had a fine time yelling obscenities at us. We travelled north and reached Bastogne in Belgium about supper time. We drove up to a large army camp that the Germans had just abandoned. The American army units had picked up about thirty Allied airmen and they had all been brought to Bastogne. There was a big dump nearby and some of the airmen were going around it, picking up German war souvenirs.

Now my worry was about sleeping in the former German camp. The Germans had just been there. They knew we were there. Maybe they'd bomb us. Of course I was jumpy about being so exposed after all those months in hiding, and knew nothing of the true course of the war. The Germans didn't bomb, they had other things on their mind. We slept in a mess hall, strewn with garbage and papers. We were given blankets and slept on the floor with about 100 U-S soldiers. The next morning we breakfasted on American rations, two square biscuits with cheese or bully beef between, washed down with hot coffee. We said our goodbyes. The thirty airmen, three Canadians, five British, the rest American, were loaded into jeeps. A motley crew. Most in bedraggled uniforms. Some in civilian clothes, just bedraggled. One of the fellows had been hiding out about forty kilometres from Etalle where I had stayed with Albert Paul and his family. One fellow, sporting a huge moustache, had hidden for a few months in a bordello in Liège. They had run a black market trade in butter he said.

Just north of Bastogne we ran into an area where the Germans had cut and dropped large trees across the highway. The American engineers were hand-cutting these. We would get out of the vehicles and the jeeps would make their way over the banks and through the bushes to get around. We drove in convoy north to a place called Huy. We travelled to Namur, using a Bailey bridge, or floating bridge that the engineers had put in place. We soon turned north west to Brussels. I didn't pinch myself. I just enjoyed the glory of it. In a daze.

Our convoy arrived in Brussels at about supper time the same day. At the Metropole Hotel! Life was certainly looking up! This was like Toronto's Royal York. It was in Brussel's main square which holds the seventeenth century statue *"Maniquin qui pisse,"* the little boy peeing into the fountain. We entered the front door and there on the right was the bar. Sitting at the first table, near the door of the bar, was none other than Major Ken Cross, along with a couple of buddies. Army Major Ken Cross, Cardy's brother-in-law. The last time I'd seen him was nine months before in December of '43 when he'd been taking training flights in the Halifax with us, in preparation for D-Day. I was in full

American uniform, with gun and steel helmet. I strolled over and said, "Ken, what the hell are you doing here?" He looked startled, smiled and said, "What are you doing in that get up?" "I'll go up and have a bath and come down, we'll have a beer," I said. We were billeted two to a room. My roommate was an American bomb aimer. Room 315. He was wearing the civvies he'd used while he was hiding out for the past couple of months. I, of course, was dressed as an American lieutenant. We bathed and cleaned up but when I came back down Cross and his army buddies were gone. At the time Cross was acting Canadian liaison officer, attached to Montgomery's army.

We went to the bar where I met a major in the American Air Force. His name was Laird and I told him about my pilot George Laird, and a sorrow that I had held at bay for months swept over me. To think of my crew, all dead. And now the war nearly over. I had told everyone I could speak French and would do the translating to increase "friendly relations." At the next table there were five lovely, blonde Belgian girls. "O.K. boy," said the Americans. "Start your talking." I made my best pitch in French, with smiles. And got the cold shoulder. Five cold shoulders. These girls were Flemish-speaking Belgians, not French-speaking. And there was no love lost between the two. My new found buddies were disgusted with me.

My roommate was undaunted. "I hear there's a dance tonight at the big hall, the other side of the square." "Ah. Good idea," was the chorus. None of us had been dancing in a long time. British General Lord Bernard Montgomery and his troops had liberated Brussels just the day before so the city was celebrating. The dance was in a large hall, and it was packed. It shut down at 11 o'clock, war-time hours.

There was no sign of my roommate. 'He's gone. Typical American,' I thought. I went down for breakfast next morning, still no roommate. He arrived just as I started to eat. "Guess where I spent the night, last night?" "Oh, I bet," I said. "No, no, no," he said. "I was in jail. The British MP's heard me saying 'Ya, Ya, Ya.' Took one look at my clothes. They thought I was a German spy and put me in jail. I've been in jail all night."

It was only now that I thought I was going to make it back to England. And only now that I could think again about family. I had been living one day at a time for so long. We were allowed one telegram home. A form telegram stating "I am alive and well." I sent this to my mother. She, in fact, never received it.

Shortly after breakfast an RAF Wing Commander ordered us into a central room in the hotel. The thirty of us. A rag tag group. Mainly in scruffy civilian clothes. Tired. Tired but hopeful. The Wing Commander took command. "I want all the guns, grenades and bombs on the table. I want all your souvenirs on the table." A large table in the middle of the floor was the only furniture in the room. I thought, 'I have the gun I had grabbed on one of our raids on German convoys under my arm pit. I'm not going to get rid of that.' My gun was a Polish-made Mador, similar to an American 45 only it was a nine millimetre. I'd already lost the souvenirs that I left with the Randolet *Maquis* group. In moments the table was loaded. I was shocked. Big potato-masher hand grenades, live German hand grenades. Two or three guys tossed in 25 calibre pistols like the rifle I had had. They had the paratrooper version. The stock folds over and you can use it like a pistol. They had four or five of those. The Wing Commander watched, non-committal until the action stopped. Then he said, "We're going to search you as you go out. And you'd better not have anything on you." I thought, 'If they search me, they search me.' But they didn't. I guess they figured they had the big stuff.

We rode the military bus to the Brussels airport, now commanded by the Allied forces. There was an American C-47 Dakota on the tarmac. It was used for paratrooper drops. All of us were taken on board, where we sat on tin seats. We were on our way home.

CHAPTER SIXTEEN

FOG HAD CLOSED IN THE LONDON AIRPORT. The pilot said, "Navigator, where are we?" The navigator looked up from the comic book he was reading. "I don't know where the hell we are." He was told to find out and be quick about it. My thought was, 'Is this the American air force?'

We landed at an American aerodrome north of London and were loaded into two trucks. We were standing in the back of the trucks for the ride into the city. It was hard to believe I was finally in England. My mind was still running with the *Maquis* in France. Then in the distance I saw a road-side tavern. I banged on the roof of the truck with both hands. The driver pulled over and called, "What's the trouble?" I shouted back, "We haven't had English beer for months. Couldn't we stop?" The trucks rolled into the tavern yard and we all went in for two or three beers. Most of us still had British money from our escape kits. The waiters kept the beer flowing and didn't worry too much about getting paid.

In London we were taken to a medical clinic for examination and delousing. We were all given new issue British battle dress, R.A.F., Americans, Canadians alike. I was determined to keep my gun. The German gun I'd managed to smuggle out of Belgium. I hid it under the new uniform stacked on the bench in the showers. When I came out of the shower, my old clothes had been taken away but my gun was still there under my new uniform. Two or three of us were in pretty bad shape and were immediately shipped to Watford hospital north of London.

I wasn't allowed out of bed the first week. I had a total of forty boils all over my body. On my neck, under my armpits and around my ankles. I had scabies, all infected. And I was suffering from malnutrition. I was in the officers' ward. About forty beds in the ward. Right across from me there was an army captain with his leg in a cast. On my left a fighter pilot and a crew member from a bomber. An airman on the other side had a body cast from his neck down to his waist. There was a major who had had his arm badly damaged. The nerves were gone. His arm was shrivelled. He seemed to be going mad. He would polish his belt, then walk up and down the ward all day long.

I asked the army captain how he broke his leg. "Oh," he said, "right here in England. My jeep failed to make a corner and we hit a brick wall." And so I asked around to the others. "Oh. I was on a motorcycle and failed to make the corner and hit a brick wall." Or some other such accident. "It's only the Air Force that's winning the war," I said with a laugh. "You guys are killing yourselves right here in England." The airman beside me in the neck to waist cast said, "For God's sakes. Tone it down. I broke my back. But it had nothing to do with my aircraft. I fell out of the second floor window of the Regent Palace Hotel in London."

At the end of the third week I was released from hospital and reported to the R.A.F. investigation section in London. They took a short report on how I had survived the six months behind enemy lines. Just a short report on what for me was a long tour behind enemy lines. The officer in charge then asked, "Do you want to continue on with another tour of duty?" I immediately answered, "Yes." I figured I knew how the Germans operated. I was optimistic that the end of the war was near. And I wanted to be in on the finish. Of course this was before the Battle of the Bulge held up the Allies in Belgium that winter. But first I was posted on a week's leave in England, with a week in Canada as well, before I would be operational.

My first stop after the debriefing was the bank in London. I hadn't drawn any pay for six months. Then I intended to head north to Leeming, to see who was about at 427 Squadron. As I waited in line at the bank I heard a voice arguing loudly with the teller at the next wicket. Sounded like the customer was overdrawn and wanted a loan. I recognized the voice. It was our gunnery leader from 427 Squadron, Rocky Durocher. And beside him was his brother Ken, a navigator at 427. I walked over. "Rocky, what are you doing here?" He turned around. "My God, Moffat, you're supposed to be dead. What are you doing here?" "Well I came back to life," I told him. He immediately said "We'll have to do a low level over London tonight. I'm just trying to get some money here." And we spent the rest of the day and night on a pub crawl. There had been a saying on squadron that if you bail out over Germany the first question you'll be asked is, "Does Rocky Durocher still hold the record time for downing a pint?" then you'll be asked your name, rank and serial number.

At Leeming I found Ganderton doing his second tour. As Wing Commander. I had long talks with him and visited a few of the pubs at Harrogate, then went back to London to the officers' club to await my boat for Canada. While there, a bomber crew came in from a forced landing near London. The flight lieutenant had been my course officer at Macdonald. A number of us heading for Canada were shipped to Warrington near Liverpool where we waited in the pouring rain for more than a week before being shipped out to North America aboard the Queen Mary. The ship was packed with American and Canadian airmen and soldiers, and their wives. The crossing was stormy, the ship was pitching in the waves, and we weren't allowed on deck. I still had to cover myself everyday with an antiseptic paste from the neck down to help heal the boils and scabies, but otherwise I was feeling great.

It was early morning as the ship came into New York harbour. I could see the statue of Liberty in the distance. I had some idea of the emotion felt by new immigrants on seeing that lady, holding the torch of liberty on high. It brought tears to my eyes. The Red Cross met us with coffee and donuts at the railway station. The R.C.A.F contingent took the train to Ottawa's Rockcliffe R.C.A.F. Station, arriving October 22, 1944.

For my family it had been a long six months with no information concerning my welfare. My mother had been called to the telephone at a neighbour's home to hear the telegram that I was missing in action. My younger brothers and sister were taken out of school to be told the news. My sister Jean, who was working in a munitions factory in Ajax during the war, remembers this call from my mother who was crying hard. "Your brother Jim is missing. But he'll come home. He'll come home." The telephone went dead. My brother Rob was at work that day cutting wood for a farmer. He stopped at the village general store on the way home and was told the news. The official notice came April 10, signed by Charles Power, Minister of National Defence for Air. "I have learned with deep regret that Flying Officer James Moffat, R.C.A.F. has been reported missing. The government and people of Canada join me in expressing the hope that more favourable news will be forthcoming in the near future." On April 22, 1944 my Wing Commander at R.A.F. Station Leeming, Bob Turnbull, wrote to my mother "...It is with deepest regret that I write to you this date to convey to you the deep feelings of my entire Squadron... We lost one of our best Crews when this aircraft did not return from this Operation and we count its loss a bitter blow to the strength of this Squadron... Jim was popular with all ranks of this Squadron's personnel and active in all Station activities... At all times he carried out his duties as an Officer and a gentleman in a most exemplary manner. We shall miss him greatly... I would like to assure you also how greatly we all honour the heroic sacrifice your son has made for the Cause of Freedom, so far from home in the Service of the British Commonwealth of Nations."

Then the long summer with no word. Many a time at least one of the younger children heard my mother crying in the dark of night. In mid-summer my father wrote to the R.C.A.F. and on August 23 the Casualty Officer for Chief of the Air Staff wrote "...no further information has been received concerning your son, Flying Officer James Moffat. Every effort is still being made to trace your son, although due to the lapse of time it is now felt there is less hope of locating him...." Exactly a month later, on September 23, that same Casualty Officer wrote "...I am pleased to inform you that the Royal Canadian Air Force Casualties Officer, Overseas, has advised me that your son, Flying Officer James Moffat, previously reported missing on Active Service, is now reported to have arrived safely in the United Kingdom on September 15th, 1944. I join with you and the members of your family in your joy in your son's safety." My mother did not receive the telegram that I had sent on or about September 14 from Brussels, Belgium until long after I had arrived home in Canada.

But well into October my family was still awaiting word about my welfare, and whereabouts. I can't believe I didn't write. My father wrote again to the R.C.A.F. "Since I received your most welcome news via wire and letter of September 16 notifying me of my son's return to U.K., I have received no further information. Could it be possible, kindly send me at least an address, whereby I can get in touch with him. And if possible his condition." Once again the Casualty Officer wrote. This time on October 27, actually five days after I had already arrived at Ottawa. "...As the cable received here advising that your son had arrived in the United Kingdom did not state that he was injured in any way, no further report would be forthcoming. However, I have dispatched an enquiry Overseas to ascertain his present well being... a letter addressed to your son c/o Royal Canadian Air Force, Overseas, will be delivered to him."

I went on leave almost immediately. I'm quite sure now that I did phone home, at least once I got to Canada. I took the train to Colborne. I had walked into town from the train station to get a taxi. It was just before seven in the morning. Coming down the street was my brother Rob in his car. He was as surprised as I was. He was meeting a crew to go picking apples, and there I was. We headed out for home. In his car, a 1930 Model A Ford. A little yellow convertible coupe, with canvas top, and a rumble seat in back. We were heading up the little curve just north of town when smoke started to roll up through the floor boards. I instinctively ducked and yelled, "There's fire. Fire." Rob said quite calmly, "That's just oil, dripping on the muffler." I replied, "Jesus Christ. Oil burns don't you know." I was ready to jump out I was so nervous. Of course the little Ford was only going about twenty miles an hour up the grade.

When I got out of the car in our yard our old farm dog Buster came running. "Oh, Buster, Buster, Buster," I called and he came to me just as though it was yesterday. We stepped into the kitchen and my mother wrapped her strong, bony arms around me.

Then came one of the most difficult things I had to do. I borrowed Rob's car and travelled to Bowmanville. I paid a visit to King Cole's mother. Twenty year old Flying Officer Kenneth Arthur Cole, air gunner in a Lancaster, 405 Squadron Grandsen Lodge, was shot down by a German fighter on the March 15, 1944 raid on Stuttgart, Germany. He was their only child. Mrs. Cole clung to me.

Of the five officers who graduated top of our class at Macdonald, Manitoba I believe only one or two of us survived. Epsted was top of the class. I think he may have survived. I haven't been able to confirm that. I was second. King Cole was third. Flying Officer Victor Stewart, with 419 Squadron at Middleton-St.George died in a fighter attack over Germany and was buried there. Flying Officer

Stan Queen was at 424 Squadron at Skipton on Swale, killed July 6, 1944, at Firacourt, France.

I took the train to Timmins. I had to see Mrs. Fournier, Roger's mother. Roger was one of a large family. A large, close family. Mrs. Fournier cried, "Why did you come back and my Roger didn't? Why didn't my Roger come back?" I couldn't answer that.

EPILOGUE

IT WAS EARLY IN JUNE OF 1987 that I received a letter from the Department of Veterans' Affairs in Ottawa to say that someone was enquiring about me. Trying to find me. A teenager on a Rotary school exchange from Belgium. The student's letter was enclosed. He wrote that he hoped I was "the" Airman Moffat. The one his grandmother Marie Claire Paul had talked about so often. Who had parachuted into Belgium during the war and been helped by his grandparents. That's how I first heard of Laurent Croughs, Vital Paul's grandson.

Laurent was attending a high school in Bracebridge, Ontario, as an exchange student sponsored by the Rotary Club of Halanzy, Belgium. He had told his history class the story his grandmother often told him, when he was a little boy. About a Canadian airmen his grandfather and great-uncle had rescued in World War II. The history teacher started the search through the Department of Veterans

Affairs. I immediately called the school and Laurent visited our home in Montreal.

And it was Laurent's wish that I return to Belgium to visit the scenes of those months behind enemy lines, fighting on the run. As luck would have it Nel Lind of the Dutch Resistance was a guest of the Royal Air Force Escaping Society, Canadian Branch that year. Her group invited forty couples for a ten day tour of Holland the next spring, in May of 1988. During the tour I called Laurent who was studying in Brussels. He asked us to cut short our visit to Holland because an event was planned for Saturday. My wife Anne and I travelled to Brussels where he met us. Over the years since 1945 I had written now and then to a few of the people involved. But not often. And not lately. It was a first reunion in forty-four years. But they didn't forget.

Laurent's brother Renaud picked us up at the train station in Arlon and drove us to Halanzy. My wife Anne had warned me that everything would be changed after all those years. But it was as if time had stood still here in the hill country. The rolling hills, the valleys, the forests, the farms clinging to the hillsides. Tears dimmed my eyes. I was returning to my second home after forty-four years. We stayed in Halanzy with Anne Paul, daughter of Vital, and mother of Laurent. She was living next door to her mother Marie-Claire where I had stayed the first night after being rescued by Vital in 1944. Anne had been seven years old then, and not allowed to see the airman being hidden in the house. Unfortunately Marie-Claire was in a convalescent home in northern Belgium, recovering from cancer. I would not meet up with her for another couple of years.

The next day a celebration was planned across the border at Quincy, France. Emile Randolet showed up. He had been driven to Halanzy by a friend of the Pauls, Joe Brembati. The last I had seen of Randolet his hat had been shot off and was flying in the wind as he ran from the German barrage at Quincy. It was while he was being treated for his wound at Vigneulles that he heard the worst about the disaster at Quincy. He wrote "It was there also that I was told by André Lambiney of the hanging of our comrades Warion and Pawlak, also of the death of Lulu." Lucien Hennekin. It was Lucien Sibéneler who let him know that I had joined the Americans in the advance toward the German border.

Brembati drove us to Quincy, to the home of Fernand Mozzo. Mozzo was the truck driver who had driven the Russians and myself back to the forest, and me on to Louis Paul's home at Baalon in 1944. He just happened to live in Quincy, the scene of our disastrous raid on the Germans. Six of the Randolet *Maquis* unit showed up for this reunion. Randolet, Denis Trussart, Robert Kesseler, Roger Broggi, Gino Norris, and Marcel Jonette. The others had died or were not able to join us. We drank a little of Mozzo's berry and rhubarb wine, then headed out for the town hall. The town of Quincy held a reception in my honour. Little glasses of wine and round loaves of plain bread. In the tradition of "breaking bread" to signify the seriousness and honour of the occasion. The mayor told the story of the twenty people, including him and his wife, being held hostage by the Germans that day. He said how glad they were that the resistance unit had not come back with more power. The Germans had said they would shoot all the hostages if that happened. He also talked of the horror of having to witness the executions of Warion and Pawluck the next morning.

We went to the flour mill. The miller and his wife, Monsieur and Madame Lemarchal were there to greet us. They and Trussart retold the story of the two *Maquis,* one of whom was Trussart, hiding in the flour bins. The miller had been afraid that he and his wife would be shot by the Germans but they hadn't revealed the hiding place. We walked along the dam and down river to where Marcel Pierre had hidden in the water.

It was Marcel Pierre who had brought me up to date on the members of the Randolet unit in 1945. In fact Marcel wrote to my parents in May of '45, searching for news of me. Wondering if I had made it through the war. He wrote "…be kind enough to give us some news of the one who was, and will always be, our fighting comrade…." In October of that same year he wrote of how the *maquisards* often spoke of me "…and knowing the shortage of cigarettes at the time (we were in the woods) we think of your comrades in the American army. We developed a taste for Camel, Chesterfield, Lucky (Strike), but now that is finished…. I send to you greetings from all *les copains…. Vive le Canada, Vive le France.* -signed Marcel. Marcel Pierre had died a couple of years before the reunion at Quincy.

After recovering from his wounds in the Quincy raid, Lieutenant Emile Randolet had returned to civilian life, taking up a teaching post, this time at Baccarat, Vosges. Lucien Sibéneler had returned to the French navy. André and Gilbert Lambinet went back to the police force. René Jacques of Jametz worked on his father's farm. Gino Norris and Marcel Jonette joined de Gaulle's First Army. They were part of the advance into Germany. Roger Broggi returned to his home in that area of France.

Our Quincy reunion party celebrated with dinner at a

nearby roadhouse. The village of Quincy has since erected a monument beside the town hall honoring Hennekin, Warion and Pawluk.

We paid a short visit to Louis Paul in Baalon. He was in a wheel chair, having lost his legs to diabetes. Louis Paul was very emotional, and cried, remembering his work with the *Maquis*. After the liberation Lieutenant Louis Paul returned to the army, guarding German prisoners of war at Guéret.

The next day the village of Rachecourt, Belgium, honoured me with a reception at the town hall. There I met Cécile Paul for the first time since jumping out her upstairs window in Etalle, forty-four years earlier. We hugged and cried. And chattered in French. And hugged some more. This was the most difficult meeting for me. Cécile had given up the most to help Bill Jones and me. She had lost the most. She had coached Bill and me in French during the day for six weeks. She had fed us out of her meagre budget, clothed us, while every day dreading the appearance of the Gestapo. There had been three German raids in Etalle during that time. Cécile's closest friend was taken away in one of these and never seen again.

And when the Gestapo did come she didn't dart out the back way to escape. Her first thought was to give us a chance. Frightened and screaming as the Gestapo were breaking down her front door she took the time to run up the stairs and warn us. Very brave for a young woman in her early twenties, holding a baby girl in her arms. It was just fortunate that in the confusion of the Germans trying to capture us Cécile was able to run next door and make her escape with the help of the Messiens. Otherwise she would have faced the same fate as her husband Albert, the firing squad. She introduced me to her second husband Joseph

Masse and her daughter Monique, the baby I had rocked to sleep so long ago. She wanted to know how soon we could come to her home in Namur, all the time we were laughing and crying, trying to bridge the gap of all those years.

I met the woman who was the little girl who dropped the egg. And her mother whose phone call had startled me so much that first night in Halanzy. They remembered it all.

Rachecourt was the crash site of the two aircraft, my Halifax and the Lancaster bomber. The villagers remembered vividly the crash of the two planes, the fourteen dead airmen, and the horrific fire that burned the Halifax and some of my crew. Again there were speeches and food, but here there were also gifts. The village gave me gifts from my aircraft. Ash trays made from part of the plane. The oxygen container. A two foot rope from the parachute cords. A little handkerchief made from my parachute silk, embroidered with the Belgian and British flags. It was a piece left over from the underwear making. And of course a T-shirt with "Rachecourt" on it.

We went to the graveyard in Halanzy with Cécile. There Vital Paul is buried beside his beloved brother Albert. It was very emotional and difficult. Albert was such a happy go lucky fellow. There were no words to say. We consoled each other.

We went then to have cocktails with Albert Paul's old Sergeant of the *gendarmerie* at Etalle. Sergeant Georges Goffinet had served in the resistance with Albert. His daughter had been a courier for their *Maquis* unit. He was retired and lived not far away from Rachecourt. There we had champagne and again something to eat.

It was on to a reunion luncheon with Madame Germaine Autphene. Her husband Major René Autphene was not well and was confined to his bed. Her brother Guy Giot, whom I had known as "Emile," had emigrated to South America and died of cancer in Brazil. Germaine had moved to Virton. For the past two days I had thought our driver Joe Brembati had been driving too fast over these narrow highways. Now Anne and I transferred to Germaine's car with a sigh of relief for the sentimental journey to Couvreux and Torgny. To our horror she not only drove too fast but drove with one hand, barely negotiating the sharp curves, waving her other hand at likely spots that I would remember. We stopped at her old school in Couvreux. At L'hermitage in Torgny. We met the Grey Nun who was living in the belfry apartment where I had hidden for a month. She had fixed it up nicely for herself. A far cry from the stark room with an old straw sack for a bed that I had been glad to have.

The Messiens greeted us at Etalle. With a luncheon of coffee and rhubarb pie. I was finding it difficult to keep my end up with the eating and drinking. The Messiens hadn't changed a bit in forty-four years. They had moved just a block away from their old home, but otherwise they seemed the same.

I remembered well the doctor who treated me for scabies, boils and malnutrition in the Belgian *Maquis* dugout, although I had never known his name. And the needle he gave me had not done much good. But it was through his advice that I was sent to Madame Adam and Madame Autphene. The doctor did not survive. He was shot by the Germans two days after treating me.

Cécile had re-married and now lived in Namur. She and her husband drove us to Namur for dinner with Monique. Baby Monique as I still thought of her.

I was now a member of the Royal Air Force Escaping Society, Canadian Branch. Each year this Society would bring members' "helpers" from Europe as guests for a holiday and the annual meeting. The fall of 1988 I sponsored my first "helper" Cécile Masse Ravé, of Namur, Belgium. Her daughter Monique accompanied her. They travelled by train to Lahr, Germany where they were flown from the former Canadian forces base to Ottawa. They spent three days in the capital city then a week with us in Montreal. Cécile and our other guests attended a reception in Quebec city given by Quebec's Lieutenant Governor Gilles Lamontagne. Lamontagne was a former navigator in the R.C.A.F. He had been shot down and spent two years in a prisoner of war camp. My guests attended the annual meeting in Toronto which included a trip to Niagara Falls.

Two years later I sponsored Marie Claire Paul and her daughter Anne Paul. I was president and our annual meeting was in Montebello Inn, Montebello, Quebec. Marie Claire remembered me clearly even though I was in her home for only one night. "Oh yes, he was such a tall man, and he had such big feet," she said. Laurent Croughs was by then a student at the University of Ottawa. I arranged for him to attend our annual banquet and so had three generations of the Paul family with me. Our son Brad, his wife Barb, and Mary McLean daughter of Angus McLean, a member and former premier of Prince Edward Island, led us in singing O Canada. A significant moment for us all. I thanked all our helpers for their courage and unstinting kindness under terrible conditions in helping us so many years ago. In 1991 Germaine Autphene, the energetic former school teacher and bee keeper came to Canada as my guest. Germaine attended our annual meeting in Niagara

Falls and visited her son at the United Nations where he worked with the Belgian delegation. This meant she came to us again before returning home. Maire Claire and Germaine have both died. I was glad to be able to recognize my brave helpers.

Bill Jones never returned to Belgium. In fact he didn't often talk to his family about his war-time experiences. But he did tell these stories. While in the German camp, near the end of the war, he and his fellow inmates managed to assemble a radio to listen to news of the Allies' advance across Europe. Each man carried a radio part, and these were assembled for brief moments only, to listen to the news. The Germans could never find an actual radio. And at one point he and his friends faked an escape attempt, just to keep the Germans on their toes. After the war, he was promoted to warrant officer and left the R.A.F. in February of 1946 after almost five years of service. Bill Jones worked as a sales representative in the engineering industry until his retirement. Monique Paul, Albert and Cécile's daughter, visited the Jones family in England and Bill's son Robert visited the Pauls in Belgium. But Bill Jones never did. He died of lung cancer in 1971.

After the war, Désire Paul received full honors for his resistance work, both from the Allies and from his hometown of Torgny. The Bureau of Investigations on Aid Given to Evading Allies, British section, in Brussels recognized his work. And le Bourgmestre of Torgny presented Désire with a certificate "that Désire Paul... has hidden at his home during the occupation by the enemy a great number of rebels and French political prisoners, a Canadian aviator (myself), four Russians and a Polish (man). In belief of that, we have presented this certificate for service and bravery..."

Vital Paul did not receive a certificate or any recognition for his long years of fighting the enemy by doing intelligence work for the Allies. Anne Paul says her father didn't apply for it. Vital Paul died of a heart attack in 1961. He never got over the execution of Albert by the Germans.

When the war in Belgium was over, and the country fully liberated, the Allies pushed into Germany. Supreme Commander of the Allied Expeditionary Force, General Dwight Eisenhower issued an "Order of the Day" to the officers and men of all Belgian Resistance Organizations, "...who in carrying out my orders, have fought so magnificently. They can be justly proud of having by their devoted heroism contributed so largely to the liberation of their beloved homeland. The rapidity of the advance of the Allied Forces which has spared much of your country the horrors of war has been due in no small measure to your help. I salute especially your honoured dead and wounded... and if you are required by your government to continue the struggle as members of the regular Belgium Armed Forces, I shall be proud to have you once more under my command...."

The British General Lord Bernard Montgomery also paid tribute to the Belgian resistance. "When the invader occupied your territory a second time, (WWI being the first time) you have shown that your spirit of resistance was living intact by engaging directly the clandestine struggle against the enemy. In my opinion, the action of the Resistance is more meritorious than that of the regular army..."

Albert Paul, a hero and martyr of the resistance, was honoured posthumously by his country. In May of 1945 he was named *Premier Maréchal des Logis*, a "first sergeant" in the *gendarmerie*. He was named an agent of the Intelligence Corps. In 1946 he was given the *"Médaille de Resistant"* by Royal Decree and recognized as *"Resistant Armé"* for the years 1943 and '44.

With the liberation, Albert's body was removed from the grim burial plot at *La Citadelle* in Liège and brought home to Halanzy in October of 1944. It was an emotional homecoming and the funeral cortège was a long one. It bore the respect for his resistance work, his long months of suffering, and the ultimate price he paid for his country, Belgium. The cortège included the *gendarmerie* from Etalle and other areas, a long list of *"Les Insoumis"* the *Maquis* units, including Halanzy and Torngy. The F.F.I, *La Fronte Francaise de l'Intérieur*, and the *gendarmerie francais*, contingents of Belgian deportees, Belgian and French soldiers of World War I, Belgian soldiers of 1940, and a delegation of the American army.

Christian Paul attended the funeral. The next day Christian wrote *"L'enterrement d'un martyr."* "Yesterday the body of Albert Paul was buried; he had been picked up by the Germans for taking in Allied parachutists. He made a number of sabotages. The body of Albert Paul was carried to the city hall. The day of the funeral everyone went to the city hall and a number of *maquisards* of the gendarmes, two American officers, some custom officers and lots of other people assisted in the mass, at the cemetery and in the cortège. In front of city hall an address was made on Albert Paul by *M. le bourgmestre* (the mayor). Again at the cemetery two addresses were made, first by the gendarmes and second by *M. le bourgmestre*. A little wooden cross bearing his name was (placed) where he was buried. The hero is my uncle and all my life I will follow his example" -signed Ch. Paul. Christian Paul was eight years old.

The 700 year old *La Citadelle Saint Walburge* in Liège is no more. It has been torn down to make way for a university hospital. Some ramparts remain. And *L"Enclos National des Fusillés de la Citadelle*. A memorial for those executed by the Germans. Row upon row of concrete crosses, painted white, bearing name plaques, still stand for those men who faced the Nazi firing squads. One of them carries the name of Albert Paul, and the date of his execution.

My visit to Belgium and France in '88 prompted a former resident of Halanzy to launch a campaign to place a monument at Rachecourt, in memory of the airmen who had died there. Arsène Martin had been an eyewitness to the crash. He worked with the mayors of the villages in the Aubange district, which includes Halanzy and Rachecourt, to raise the money.

Two days before March 31, 1990 I found myself in a hotel in Arlon, Belgium. I travelled to the cemetery at Arlon to visit the grave of Jock Morrison, our flight engineer on that last operation. Flying Officer Jock Morrison D.F.C. of the Royal Air Force. Morrison had landed in the trees. The Germans took him to the hospital in Arlon where he died 20 days after the crash.

The other crew members of the two aircraft were dead at the crash site. In September of 1945 the R.C.A.F. found that the official German *"totenliste"* number 220 recorded the burial place of the deceased crew members in the military cemetery, Florennes Jusaine, just south east of Florennes, Belgium. They were all re-buried in the British military cemetery at Hotton, on the Belgian-Luxembourg border.

Canada had recognized my pilot's bravery in two ways. Squadron Leader George J. Laird had won the D.F.C. for saving wounded flight engineer Cardy by insisting on bringing down our damaged plane, rather than bailing out. And in 1958, The Canadian Board of Geographical Names named a peninsula in Frobisher Bay, Laird Peninsula. Sergeant Bill Cardy had received the Conspicuous Gallantry Medal for his part in bringing the plane down safely, while seriously injured. After his recovery in hospital Cardy returned to Canada.

I took a taxi from Arlon to Rachecourt. I was amazed to see about 200 people walking up the main street. Marie-Claire and Anne Paul were in the lead. Arm in arm. Four or five people were carrying flags. And there was a band. It was a parade to the front of the town hall. On the steps was a party of dignitaries, including Canada's air attaché to Brussels, a representative of the British air attaché, the local member of the Belgian parliament, and Mayor Francois Rits of Halanzy. I stood beside the draped stele that had been erected at the front of the town hall.

Mayor Rits told how Arsène Martin had seen the light from the fire and heard the explosions the night of the crash. He had run through the meadows to one of the burning aircraft. He looked with horror at the burned bodies lying face down in the ploughed field. Their parachutes still closed on their backs. At the other aircraft the turret had crashed, trapping the gunner in the twisted metal. Mayor Rits closed his speech with these words, "And now, to these brave soldiers, victims of war, may I be allowed to say, in the name of all, wholeheartedly and simply, that the inhabitants of Rachecourt will never forget: This monument will prove it forever."

I unveiled the stele which carries the names of the crew members of both bombers, the R.C.A.F. Halifax and R.A.F. Lancaster, with the date March 31, 1944. It was forty-five years to the day. I spoke these words in English and French.

"It is a great privilege and pleasure for me to be here today for the official inauguration of this stele erected in memory of the English and Canadian airmen who fell at Rachecourt on the night of March 31,1944.

The fact that the community of Aubange and the people of Rachecourt took the time and expense to honour these airmen touches me very deeply. This stele will keep alive the names of these airmen for future generations.

I now invite you to project your thoughts into the future when the grandchildren of your grandchildren learn of the reasons why these airmen are listed here, how they arrived in their ungainly aircraft, the terrible collision and their deaths. Yes - they died - so that we could have Peace and Justice. Almost fifty hears later, all of us assembled here are witnesses to this. After the many changes in Europe and in the world, in recent months, perhaps we can dare to hope this will be the last stele necessary.

On behalf of my crew remembered here and their families, and for the airmen of the British aircraft and their families, I thank you most sincerely for what you have done here today. God Bless all of you."

Message given by: Flying Officer James Moffat (retired) R.C.A.F. Sole survivor of this collision.

James Moffat was de-mobbed from the Royal Canadian Air Force in March of 1945. He attended rehab school at Ryerson in Toronto graduating in 1946. He started civilian life with the Bata Shoe Company, then went into business with Household Finance Corporation at Brantford, Ontario in 1946 moving to Ottawa, Brockville and finally Montreal. Moffat spent thirty-seven and a half years with Household Finance, most of it at the premier office in downtown Montreal. He retired in Montreal in 1984. He and his wife, Anne, had six children, two of whom died, one at two days old and one in a traffic accident at twenty years of age. James Moffat is a life member of the Royal Air Force Escaping Society, Canadian Branch, and was president in 1989 and 1990. Rik Craeghs of the Belgian Resistance Society presented the Belgian Resistance Medal to Moffat at a Montreal ceremony. He is a member of the Caterpillar Club. In his lapel Moffat wears a tiny, three-quarters inch caterpillar pin. It is gold-plated, ruby-eyed, and priceless. On the back is engraved his name, rank, and serial number. The caterpillar is awarded by the Irwin Airchute Company to anyone who has had his life saved by a parachute. James Moffat is a life member of the Air Gunners Association. He belongs to the Bomber Command Association, Air Crew Association, R.C.A.F. Association, and 427 Squadron Association. Moffat is also a life member and trustee of the Yorkshire Air Museum, Elvington, Yorkshire, England Canada Branch. He is a member of the Canadian Aviation Historical Society. And he's had a life interest in biking, swimming and playing bridge, sailing and cross country skiing.

APPENDIX

Aircraft	Crew	Target
Operation One - 5 Sept, 1943 Halifax, W-Willy	Pilot F/L George Laird, nav Sgt George Lorimer, b/a Sgt Joe Corbally, wag Sgt Pat Clapham RAF, f/e Sgt Bill Cardy, mu/ag P/O James Moffat, r/ag F/O Jack Findlay	Mannheim, Ger. 7:10 hrs* dco**
Operation Two - 22 September, 1943 Halifax, W-Willy	Pilot F/L George Laird, nav Sgt George Lorimer, b/a Sgt Joe Corbally, wag Sgt Pat Clapham RAF, f/e Sgt Bill Cardy, mu/ag P/O James Moffat, r/ag F/O Jack Findlay	Hanover, Ger. 5:40 hrs dco

Operation Three - 3 October, 1943 Halifax, W - LK637	Pilot F/L George Laird, nav Sgt George Lorimer, b/a Sgt Joe Corbally, wag F/O Jack Rogerson RAF, f/e Sgt Bill Cardy, mu/ag P/O James Moffat, r/ag F/O Jack Findlay	Kassell, Ger. 4:15 hrs dnco***
Operation Four - 3 November, 1943 Halifax, W-Willy LK965	Pilot F/L George Laird DFC, co-pilot F/O Matherly, nav Sgt George Lorimer, b/a F/Sgt Joe Corbally, wag Sgt Pat Clapham RAF, f/e F/O Paddy McClune RAF, mu/ag F/Sgt Lloyd Smith, r/ag P/O James Moffat	Dusseldorf, Ger. 6:35 hrs dco
Operation Five - 22 November, 1943 Halifax, W-Willy LK965	Pilot S/L George Laird DFC, co-pilot F/S C.B. Coathup, nav F/O Red Soeder, b/a WO1 Joe Corbally, wag Sgt Pat Clapham RAF, f/e F/O Paddy McClune RAF, mu/ag F/Sgt Lloyd Smith, r/ag F/O James Moffat	Berlin, Ger. 7:05 hrs dco

Operation Six - 25 November, 1943 Halifax, W-Willy LK965	Pilot S/L George Laird DFC, co-pilot F/O Shannon, nav. Sgt George Lorimer, b/a WO1 Joe Corbally, wag Sgt Pat Clapham RAF, f/e F/O Paddy McClune RAF, mu/ag F/Sgt Lloyd Smith, r/ag F/O James Moffat	Frankfurt, Ger 7:00 hrs dco
Operation Seven - 20 December, 1943 Halifax, W-Willy LK965	Pilot S/L George Laird DFC, co-pilot F/Sgt A.R. Clibbery, nav F/O Red Soeder, b/a WO1 Joe Cor- bally, wag Sgt Pat Clapham RAF, f/e F/O Paddy McClune RAF, mu/ag F/Sgt Lloyd Smith, r/ag F/O James Moffat	Frankfurt, Ger 6:35 hrs dco
Operation Eight - 20 January, 1944 Halifax, V-Victor DK268	Pilot S/L George Laird DFC, co-pilot WO1 Major, nav F/O W.E.P.(Red) Soeder, b/a WO1 Joe Corbally, wag Sgt Pat Clapham RAF, f/e F/O Paddy McClune RAF, mu/ag F/Sgt Lloyd Smith, r/ag F/O James Moffat	Berlin, Ger. 4:30 hrs

Operation Nine - 19 February, 1944 Halifax, Mark III W-Willy LV836	Pilot S/L George Laird DFC, co-pilot F/O Weicker, nav F/O W.E.P. (Red) Soeder, b/a WO1 Joe Corbally, wag Sgt. Pat Clapham RAF, f/e F/O Paddy McClune RAF, mu/ag F/Sgt Lloyd Smith, r/ag F/O James Moffat	Leipzig, Ger. 7:15 hrs dco
Operation Ten - 25 February, 1944 Halifax, P Mark III LV831	Pilot S/L George Laird DFC, co-pilot Sgt Miller, nav F/O Red Soeder, b/a WO1 Joe Corbally, wag Sgt Pat Clapham RAF, f/e Paddy McClune RAF, mu/ag F/Sgt Lloyd Smith, r/ag F/O James Moffat	Augsberg, Ger. 8:00 hrs dco
Operation Eleven - 7 March, 1944 Halifax, P Mark III LV831	Pilot S/L George Laird DFC, Co-pilot Group Capt Bryans, (CO RAF Stn Leem- ing) nav F/O Red Soeder, b/a WO1 Joe Corbally, wag F/Sgt Pat Clapham RAF, f/e f/O Paddy McClune RAF, mu/ag f/Sgt Lloyd Smith, r/ag F/O James Moffat	Le Mans, Fr. 5:25 hrs dco

Operation Twelve - 18 March, 1944 Halifax, W-Willy LV789	Pilot S/L George Laird DFC, co-pilot P/O Devereaux, nav F/O Red Soeder, b/a WO1 Joe Corbally, wag f/Sgt Pat Clapham RAF, f/e P/O Jock Morrison DFC RAF, mu/ag F/Sgt Lloyd Smith, r/ag F/O James Moffat	Frankfurt, Ger. 5:45 hrs dco
Operation Thirteen- 30 March, 1944 Halifax, W-Willy LV923	Pilot S/L George Laird DFC, co-pilot F/Sgt Arthur Stainton, nav. F/O Red Soeder, b/a P/O Joe Corbally, wag F/Sgt Pat Clapham RAF, f/e F/O Jock Morrison DFC RAF, mu/ag P/O Lloyd Smith, r/ag F/O James Moffat	Nuremburg, Ger. dco missing****

---

nav—*navigator*   b/a—*bomb aimer*
wag—*wireless air gunner*   f/e—*flight engineer*
mu/ag—*mid upper air gunner*   r/ag—*rear air gunner*

---

* *duration of operation*   *** *duty not carried out*
** *duty carried out*   **** *missing*

Letter dated 5 September, 1945, addressed to No. 2 Section (Belgium) M.R. & E. Service, Royal Air Force Unit, Brussels, from J.S. Harris Wing, Commander for Air Officer Commanding-in-Chief, R.C.A.F Overseas: "...captured German documents reveal the other aircraft (in the Halifax crash) to be Lancaster UK.III N.D. 767 "B," (R.A.F.) which was reported missing 31 March, 1944. A statement made by F/O J. Moffat, the only survivor, corroborates the fact that his aircraft collided with another. The crew of this second aircraft consisted of the following personnel:

P/O E. Picken, pilot
P/O J.P. Meritt, nav.
Sgt. R.J. Asplin, WO/ag.
F.Sgt C.J. Schmidt, a/bomb.
Sgt. G.R. Collins, ag
Sgt. N.J. Coup, ag
Sgt. H.F. Page, f/eng.

****Missing due to mid-air collision with Lancaster from RAF 622 Squadron piloted by P/O E. Pickin. They were bomber aircraft numbers 89 and 90 lost that night. Sole survivor of both aircraft, F/O James Moffat. Total aircraft lost that night, 108. Losses 11.9 percent.

BIBLIOGRAPHY

Bomber Command War Diaries, Martin Middlebrook & Chris Everitt, Viking Penguin, New York, U.S.A., 1985.

The Nuremburg Raid, Martin Middlebrook, Fontana/Collins, 1975.

Extract from The Canadian Encyclopedia, Hurtig Publishers, Edmonton, Alta, 1988.

Fortunes in the Ground, Michael Barnes, Boston Mills Press, Erin, On, 1986.

Belgium, Margot Lyon, Thames and Hudson, London, England, 1971.

Belgium and Luxembourg, the Rough guide, Rough G. Ltd, London, England, 1997.

Resistance, edited by Russell Smith, Time-Life, 1979.

Heroes of the Resistance, editors of Army Times, Dodd, Mead & Co., New York, 1967.

Introduction to Belgium, Michael Winch, Methuen and Co. Ltd., London, 1964.

Extract from *Héros et Martyrs*, M. Paul and M.G. Levy, Brussels: editions J. Rozez, 1947.

Extract from *Hommage aux Fusillés*, G. Maillard, Liège, edition: *Liège belle époque*, 1955.

Extract from *Liège a Travers les Ages: Les rues de Liège, Vol.1 & Vol. 2*, Thomas Gobert, 1924/1975, Belgium.

Journals of the Belgium *Maquis, Les Insoumis d'Athus, Les Insoumis de Halanzy, 1940 to 1945*.

Extract from *Collectif,* published by *"commission historique de la résistance* (Belgian defence ministry), Brussels: edition Leclerq, 1948.

Extract from *Major Dufour et les siens*, F. Gerard, unpublished manuscript.

Extract from *Liège Libre Journal*, 1944 to 1994 edited by Centre de Liègois d'Histoire et *d'Archéologie Militaires, Liège*, Belgium, 1994.